MAKE YOUR VOICE HEARD

— IN —

HEAVEN

BARRY C. BLACK

The nonfiction imprint of
Tyndale House Publishers, Inc.

Visit Tyndale online at www.tyndale.com.

Visit Tyndale Momentum online at www.tyndalemomentum.com.

TYNDALE, Tyndale Momentum, and Tyndale's quill logo are registered trademarks of Tyndale House Publishers, Inc. The Tyndale Momentum logo is a trademark of Tyndale House Publishers, Inc. Tyndale Momentum is the nonfiction imprint of Tyndale House Publishers, Inc., Carol Stream, Illinois.

Make Your Voice Heard in Heaven: How to Pray with Power

Designed by Dean H. Renninger

For information about special discounts for bulk purchases, please contact Tyndale House Publishers at csresponse@tyndale.com, or call 1-800-323-9400.

Library of Congress Cataloging-in-Publication Data
Names: Black, Barry C., author.
Title: Make your voice heard in heaven : how to pray with power / Barry C. Black.
Description: Carol Stream, Illinois : Tyndale House Publishers, Inc., 2017. | Includes
    bibliographical references.
Identifiers: LCCN 2017039695 | ISBN 9781496429490 (hc)
Subjects: LCSH: Prayer—Christianity.
Classification: LCC BV220 .B53 2017 | DDC 248.3/2—dc23 LC record available at https://
    lccn.loc.gov/2017039695

Printed in the United States of America

24   23   22   21   20   19   18
7   6   5   4   3   2   1

CONTENTS

INTRODUCTION

In our "connected" society, we work to make our voices heard on earth. We tweet and blog, post videos to YouTube, and use various other forms of social media to get the word out—whatever that word might be. Here in Washington, DC, where I work, people march, lift placards, and petition Congress, hoping their voices will be heard and will make a difference.

Whenever I see people gathering together to make their voices heard, I'm reminded of the promise in Matthew 18:20 that whenever even two or three are gathered in the name of Jesus, he is in their midst. As followers of Jesus, we need to realize that when we come together to pray, we invite the palpable presence of Almighty God, and we make our voices heard in heaven.

I know there are some who say that the efficacy of prayer does not extend beyond the interior life of the one who prays. "Prayer may change *us*," or so their logic goes, "but it doesn't change anything else." But I'm more inclined to agree with Alfred Lord Tennyson, both in principle and prescription:

> *More things are wrought by prayer*
> *Than this world dreams of. Wherefore, let thy voice*
> *Rise like a fountain . . . night and day.*
> *For what are men . . .*
> *If, knowing God, they lift not hands of prayer*
> *Both for themselves and those who call them friend?[1]*

In prayer, I believe humanity cooperates with divinity. As we bring our souls into alignment with the Creator of every good thing, we avail ourselves of God's goodness, wisdom, and power. Moreover, there are things we will never receive except by request only—blessings that hang on the silken cords of prayer.

James 4:2 (NKJV) says, "You do not have because you do not ask." Moreover, we must pray believing, as Abraham did, that whatever God has promised, he is also able to perform.[2]

When Jesus went to his hometown, as recorded in Mark 6, the people there were skeptical of him.

> They asked, "Where did he get all this wisdom
> and the power to perform such miracles?" Then
> they scoffed, "He's just a carpenter, the son of
> Mary and the brother of James, Joseph, Judas,

and Simon. And his sisters live right here among us." They were deeply offended and refused to believe in him.

Then Jesus told them, "A prophet is honored everywhere except in his own hometown and among his relatives and his own family." And because of their unbelief, he couldn't do any miracles among them except to place his hands on a few sick people and heal them. And he was amazed at their unbelief.[3]

Mark 6:5 is one of the most startling Bible verses I know: "Because of their unbelief, he couldn't do any miracles among them." It doesn't say he *wouldn't* do any miracles; it says he *couldn't* do any miracles. Such is the dampening effect of unbelief. On the other hand, Jesus says that if we have faith "even as small as a mustard seed," we can move mountains.[4] Such is the power of making our voices heard in heaven.

When we lift our voices to heaven, it makes an unmistakable difference. So how do we do that?

First of all, we must pray from a sense of *need*. God instructs us through the psalmist Asaph: "Call upon me in the day of trouble; I will deliver you, and you shall glorify me."[5] When I was a young man, I used to have about forty-five seconds of prayer material. It wasn't that I didn't have needs, but I often didn't recognize them as prayer worthy. Then I got married and became a parent—and suddenly I had *plenty* of prayer material.

God wants us to pray when we *need* him. And in our day and age—with everything happening in our nation and around the world—we don't have to look very far to see our need for God. At the same time, we're not to worry. In Philippians 4:6, the Bible says, "Have no anxiety about anything, but pray about everything—with thanksgiving."[6]

When Jesus prayed his wonderful intercessory prayer in the upper room the night before he was crucified, the Bible tells us "he lifted his eyes to heaven and said, 'Father, the hour has come. Glorify your Son that your Son also might glorify you. As you have given him power to give to as many as would receive him eternal life. And this is life eternal, that they might know you—Abba, Daddy—and Jesus Christ, whom you have sent.'"[7] God wants to have an intimate relationship with us, in which we come to him as our Father, and our voices are heard in the courts of heaven.

Why do we pray?

We pray to "acknowledge that the LORD is God! He made us, and we are his. We are his people, the sheep of his pasture."[8] We also pray because we share mutual interests with him. Jesus said, "As the Father has sent me, so I am sending you."[9] Moreover, we pray because we and God have a mutual enemy. "Be sober, be vigilant; because your adversary the devil walks about like a roaring lion, seeking whom he may devour."[10]

For whom do we pray?

The apostle Paul instructs us: "I urge you, first of all, to pray for all people. Ask God to help them; intercede on their behalf, and give thanks for them. Pray this way for kings and all who are in authority so that we can live peaceful and quiet lives marked by godliness and dignity. This is good and pleases God our Savior, who wants everyone to be saved and to understand the truth."[11]

We should pray with the knowledge that we have been invited to speak to our omniscient, omnipresent, and omnipotent God. When our prayers are directed toward the enhancement of God's name and the accomplishment of his purposes, we can expect that our voices will be heard in heaven. When our prayers are heard in heaven, our need for guidance, strength, healing, mercy, grace, and wisdom will be met by the God who has given us this promise: "All glory to God, who is able, through his mighty power at work within us, to accomplish infinitely more than we might ask or think."[12] We can pray with effectiveness, even when it seems that God is silent. We can pray every prayer expecting divine assistance.

Shortly after the 2016 presidential election, I was approached by two senators as I walked into the US Capitol building one morning. You may forgive my brief anxiety, but at first it seemed as if it might be an intervention.

But I calmed myself with the truth that I had been their chaplain for nearly fourteen years, and their true purpose soon became clear.

"Barry," one of the senators said, "we would like you to deliver the keynote address at our 2017 National Prayer Breakfast."

Did I hear that correctly? Was he really talking to me?

The annual prayer breakfast, which was started during the Eisenhower administration, is an iconic event that attracts US leaders, heads of state, members of Parliament, and other luminaries from around the world. Past keynote addresses have been given by the likes of Billy Graham, Bishop Fulton Sheen, and even Mother Teresa. Was I now being offered that privilege?

I heard myself say, "Senator, I'd be delighted to serve in any way you deem helpful," but I projected far more confidence than I felt. Even as I spoke those optimistic words, I sought to be heard in heaven, whispering silently this prayer: "Lord, I surely do need you. And I need you *now*."

With about three months to prepare, I began to sleep, eat, think, walk, and talk about prayer. The book you are now holding is the result of those three months of ruminating, agonizing, and organizing. Having practiced these principles in my own private prayer life and in my role as chaplain of the US Senate, I offer my observations and advice about how to pray with power and make your voice heard in heaven.

1

PRAY WITH ASSISTANCE

If two of you agree here on earth concerning anything you ask,
my Father in heaven will do it for you. For where two or three
gather together as my followers, I am there among them.

MATTHEW 18:19-20

On July 7, 2003, I began work as the sixty-second chaplain of the United States Senate. When I walked into my Capitol Hill office for the first time, with its mesmerizing view of the Washington Monument standing majestically on the Mall, my eyes traced a path beyond it to where shimmering sunlight glinted on the surface of the reflecting pool that provides a mirror for the Lincoln Memorial. The memorial's stately pillars brought to mind Dr. Martin Luther King's involvement in the 1963 March on Washington, when he aroused the nation's conscience by articulating his dream of freedom and equality. How fortunate I was to now have a job that provided me with an office from which I could gaze upon such beauty and have a front-row seat to human history.

I surveyed the beautiful mahogany bookcases that would soon provide a residence for my personal library—allowing my mentors to join me in my work: Aristotle, Epictetus, Boethius, Kant, Hume, Spinoza, Adler, Augustine, Aurelius, and Aquinas, to name a few. They had been my companions since my sojourn to college in Alabama in the 1960s, and subsequently traveled with me to eleven churches I pastored and on numerous military deployments. They wouldn't forsake me now. I felt very much at home.

As chaplain for the upper chamber of America's legislative branch of government, I offer an invocation at the convening of each new session of the Senate. This is a wonderful opportunity to frame the day for the members, using a one-minute prayer to remind them of the importance of the spiritual, moral, ethical, and religious aspects of their work. I view this prayer as a conversation with God, evolving from the overflow of my daily devotional reading, my pastoral outreach to the thousands on the Senate side of Capitol Hill, and my daily commitment to "practice the presence" of our transcendent God.

I remember my knees knocking together the first time I ascended the steps to the Senate podium as a guest chaplain, trying to forget that countless viewers would be watching me on C-SPAN 2, in addition to the august assembly in the Senate chambers. But knowing that I would be speaking to the sovereign God of the universe, and that my voice would be heard in heaven, I felt less intimidated by my immediate surroundings, enabling me to enjoy my guest-chaplain responsibilities.

But on that July day, as I stood nervously on the Senate floor, listening to Senator Ted Stevens of Alaska, the president pro tempore, gavel me in, I was no longer a *guest* chaplain; this was my new calling.

"The Senate will now come to order," Senator Stevens intoned. "The chaplain, Dr. Barry Black, will lead the Senate in prayer."

As I began my first prayer, I once again experienced reverential awe in light of the privilege I had to speak to God on behalf of the Senate and our nation. The sound of my voice, a natural baritone I've had since puberty, brought a soothing rush of relief as the words of the prayer flowed easily. I found myself thinking, *This may work out just fine.*

With my inaugural prayer, my purpose was to announce a new beginning, celebrate God's sovereignty, acknowledge the contributions of my predecessor, Dr. Lloyd Ogilvie, encourage bipartisan cooperation, and challenge our lawmakers to reach out to the marginalized—to the lost, last, lonely, least, and left out. My fervent hope was that all this would be accomplished with a standard of excellence—as captured in the words of the apostle Paul: "I pray that . . . you will keep on growing in knowledge and understanding. For I want you to understand what really matters, so that you may live pure and blameless lives."[1]

Help from Heaven

Living pure and blameless lives is not something we come by naturally. The Bible says we were conceived in sin and "brought forth in iniquity."[2] In the words of the apostle Paul, "I know that nothing good lives in me, that is, in my sinful nature. I want to do what is right, but I can't."[3] The good we desire to do, we often don't do. The evil we hate, we find ourselves doing. We encounter a civil war inside of ourselves, and we cry out with Paul, "Wretched man that I am! Who will deliver me from this body of death?"[4]

Fortunately, we serve an all-wise God who "knows our frame" and "remembers that we are dust."[5] God knows we need help, and he has not left us unprepared.

Jesus, during his last days on earth, knowing that his disciple Peter would be tested, said to him, "I have prayed for you that your faith may not fail."[6] Imagine the leverage of having God's Son interceding on our behalf. Well, according to the book of Hebrews, we don't have to imagine it—because it's true! What Jesus did for Peter, he continues to do for us today.[7] Thank God for this assistance, because as humans we indeed have infirmities. We have blind spots and often act in ignorance. As Jesus prayed for those who crucified him, "Father, forgive them, for they don't know what they are doing."[8] Those who drove the nails into his hands did so in ignorance.

We're born with these blind spots and shortcomings. Some of us are born with physical infirmities, and all of us are born with moral weaknesses. Hereditary moral infirmity may be what "visiting the iniquity of the fathers on the children to the third and the fourth generation" means in Exodus 20:5 (ESV). Our infirmities can be exacerbated by poor education, bad habits, and other negative environmental factors. Praise God that the Holy Spirit is willing to help us with our infirmity.[9]

Think about how, throughout human history, God has helped humanity with its infirmities. He helped Moses, who murdered a man in a fit of rage. He helped Peter with his impulsiveness and vacillating. He helped Saul of Tarsus with his misplaced zeal, and Thomas with his doubting, and he unburdened Mary Magdalene of the oppression of seven devils. God also empowers *us* to "grow in the grace and knowledge of our Lord and Savior Jesus Christ"[10] so that we may overcome our hereditary and cultivated tendencies to sin.

New Beginnings

God not only helps us in our weakness, but he also gives us a fresh start when we turn to him in faith. He is the author of new beginnings, as declared in the very first verse of Scripture: "In the beginning God created. . . ."[11] The apostle John speaks of the Creator's power with these words: "All things were made through him, and without him was not any thing made that was made."[12]

God's authorship of beginnings means that we can trust him to have a plan for what he starts—even the varied journeys of our lives. In Jeremiah 29:11, God says, "I know the plans I have for you." Imagine that. The sovereign, omnipotent, and omniscient God of the universe has a detailed strategy for each of our lives. I found this promise to be very reassuring as I began my service as chaplain of the Senate, confident that God would choreograph my new vocational journey, just as he would guide the steps of the legislators I now served—*if* we would but acknowledge his sovereignty.

> Trust in the LORD with all your heart;
>   do not depend on your own understanding.
> Seek his will in all you do,
>   and he will show you which path to take.[13]

I knew I had so much to learn, but I clung to the prophet Zechariah's admonition: "Do not despise these small beginnings, for the LORD rejoices to see the work begin."[14] Yes, I had little experience in the legislature, but I served a God who equips people to walk through the doors of opportunity he opens. He gave Joseph and Daniel the ability to interpret dreams, he provided Samson with remarkable strength, and he blessed David with amazing hand-eye coordination. He gave Esther great beauty and courage, equipping her for an assignment to help her people escape the genocidal intentions of Haman.[15]

When I remembered how Jacob, Moses, and David started as humble shepherds and God splendidly used them for his glory, I became more optimistic about what God could do through me. I recalled that when Jesus chose his disciples, he didn't select them from among the aristocracy but from the blue-collar ranks.[16] That was *my* echelon, making me feel optimistic about what the future might hold.

Striving for Excellence

In my first prayer before the Senate, I wanted to mention the indispensability of *excellence*, establishing this value as a motif in subsequent prayers. Excellence has to do with finding the superior path, a practice that is certainly needed by lawmakers. It usually entails striving for great preparation, expending one's energies in a worthy cause, seizing life's opportunities, and refusing to settle for less than our best.

As I reflected on the attribute of excellence, my mind wandered back to the events of May 6, 1954, when Englishman Roger Bannister ran the first sub-four-minute mile. Many people at the time believed it couldn't be done, that it was a physiological impossibility, but Bannister did it nonetheless, recording a time of 3:59.4. What's interesting is that his record stood for only forty-six days before Australian John Landy lowered it to 3:57.9. Over the next five years, another twenty runners bested Bannister's mark as well.[17] Today, sub-fours have become almost commonplace among elite distance runners—which would seem to suggest that the standard of excellence was set too low to begin with.

In the Bible, when Daniel and his friends were examined by King Nebuchadnezzar after they had completed three years of specialized training, the monarch found them far superior to any of the other students in the program. "Whenever the king consulted them in any matter requiring wisdom and balanced judgment, he found them ten times more capable than any of the magicians and enchanters in his entire kingdom."[18] Could it be that the standard for excellence is actually that high? If it is, we all must do more to passionately pursue God's best. One way we can do that is by praying with God's assistance.

We need God's assistance when we pray because we don't know the future. We can't see even one hour ahead. I remember talking to a friend who was contemplating an assignment that would take six years to complete. But we had no idea that he would die eleven days later. The Bible says, "Do not boast about tomorrow, for you do not know what a day may bring."[19]

We also need assistance with our prayers because we rarely know what is best for us. In the eleventh grade,

I asked God to make a certain young lady fall in love with me so that we would eventually marry. I'm certainly glad that God didn't answer in the way I had hoped. I didn't know what was best for my life, but he did.

The mother of James and John came to Jesus, requesting that her sons be permitted to sit on his right and left in the new Kingdom.[20] Jesus responded, "You don't know what you are asking!"[21] You see, Jesus had no intention of setting up an earthly kingdom, as the disciples' mother (and others) had assumed, and what she requested would probably bring martyrdom to her sons. So often, we really don't know what is best. We're like children who get upset because our parents won't let us play with knives, when all our parents are trying to do is keep us from harm.

We also need to pray with assistance because two are stronger than one. "Two people are better off than one, for they can help each other succeed. If one person falls, the other can reach out and help. But someone who falls alone is in real trouble."[22] Moreover, Jesus declared, "If two of you agree here on earth concerning anything you ask, my Father in heaven will do it for you."[23]

We also need to pray with assistance because God's Spirit is willing to intercede for us. Romans 8:26-27 puts it this way: "The Holy Spirit helps us in our weakness. For example, we don't know what God wants us to pray for. But the Holy Spirit prays for us with groanings that cannot be expressed in words. And the Father who knows all hearts knows what the Spirit is saying, for the Spirit pleads for us believers in harmony with God's own will." What a marvelous way to ensure that our voices are heard in heaven! When the Holy Spirit pleads our case, we can be certain that God's purposes for our lives will prevail.

We need to pray with assistance because it enables us to follow God's strategy for praying with power. We can take advantage of the sympathy and help that God provides to remedy our defects. In the Lord's Prayer, Jesus provided his disciples with seven petitions.[24] When we pray the "Our Father," we are praying God's Word. It is God who takes the initiative in causing us to even desire to pray: "For God is working in you, giving you the desire and the power to do what pleases him."[25] Then the Holy Spirit, through God's Word, reveals God's will to us. With the aid of scriptural inspiration, we pray according to God's will. We find ourselves responding to what God is impressing upon our hearts, giving him the courtesy of starting the conversation and assisting us in our prayers.

When we pray before an open Bible, we receive assistance as we cry out with Samuel, "Speak, for your servant is listening."[26] I can tell you that praying with the assistance of Scripture and the Holy Spirit has energized my prayer life.

We need to pray with assistance because we cannot grasp God's infinite plan with our finite minds. In Isaiah, God reminds us, "My thoughts are not your thoughts, neither are your ways my ways. . . . For as the heavens are higher than the earth, so are my ways higher than your ways and my thoughts than your thoughts."[27] In the final analysis, perhaps we would do best to pray Jesus' last prayer on Calvary: "Father, into your hands I commit my Spirit!"[28]

Just as I Am

The knowledge that God offers us divine assistance with our prayers should motivate us to come to him just as we are to receive his gifts and blessings. I know of no better way to do this than to "stupid-proof" our lives by praying for the wisdom that God makes available upon request. James says, "If you need wisdom, ask our generous God, and he will give it to you. He will not rebuke you for asking."[29] I marvel at this promise, for wisdom covers every critical area of our lives, and we need it in order to live well. We don't have to go forth in our own strength. God's Spirit will help us in all of life's seasons.

When we appeal to God for wisdom, he promises to generously provide it. In short, we'll receive *more* than we need, but we must ask without doubting. The Bible says, "Let him ask in faith, with no doubting, for the one who doubts is like a wave of the sea that is driven and tossed by the wind. For that person must not suppose that he will receive anything from the Lord; he is a double-minded man, unstable in all his ways."[30] Faith, then, is a critical force in receiving God's wisdom and in making our voices heard in heaven.

Without God's wisdom, how can we live well or pray with power, particularly when we realize how little we actually know? When we, with great faith, make a request of God for wisdom, he will provide us with all that is necessary to make our voices heard in heaven and for living lives that will glorify him. This is the assistance from heaven we need in order to pray with power.

With the assistance of the Holy Spirit, I daily attempt to remind our lawmakers of God's providential power over the course of the nation—and the nations. It's not enough to have a strong military or competent governmental branches; we must look to God as the source of our nation's ultimate survival and success. "Unless the LORD builds the house, those who build it labor in vain. Unless the LORD watches over the city, the watchman stays awake in vain."[31] What is true for houses and cities is true for nations as well. Proverbs 14:34 says, "Godliness makes a nation great, but sin is a disgrace to any people." Unrighteousness, therefore, is a national security issue.

Because righteousness emerges more from unity than division, from concord than discord, I encourage our lawmakers to build bridges, to find common ground. The Bible says, "How good and pleasant it is when God's people live together in unity!"[32]

True unity usually entails a humility that esteems

others as better than ourselves[33] and is "quick to listen, slow to speak, and slow to get angry."[34] It's a humility that reflects bipartisan cooperation, which the American framers attempted to build into the upper chamber of our government's legislative branch, where a simple majority would usually be insufficient to win the day.

My first prayer as Senate chaplain was also about the inescapable laws of sowing and reaping. In our work, we may plant and water, but God gives the increase. As Paul writes, "I planted the seed in your hearts, and Apollos watered it, but it was God who made it grow."[35] I wanted to remind our lawmakers of the certainty of a harvest if they persevered in doing what is right. "Let's not get tired of doing what is good. At just the right time we will reap a harvest of blessing if we don't give up."[36]

In this planting of seeds, encounters with unproductive soil could bring discouragement. When some seeds fall on hard, rocky, or thorny soil, it might engender in the sower a cynicism and despair. But it's all just part of the process. "As long as the earth remains, there will be planting and harvest, cold and heat, summer and winter, day and night."[37] Our responsibility is to persevere in praying with God's assistance.

This sowing and reaping also requires that we seek the wisdom of the Lord of the harvest. Like all of us, our lawmakers shouldn't lean primarily on their own wisdom, but instead should trust in a God who knows the future and has promised to direct their steps. "Seek his will in all you do, and he will show you which path to take."[38]

I felt such spiritual strength as I attempted to depend on God's Spirit to help me write my initial prayer. How I wanted our lawmakers to focus on being faithful. The issue is always one of fidelity to God, regardless of how our circumstances play out. I wanted them to permit praises to go up so that blessings could come down, for God is "enthroned on the praises" of his people.[39] I wanted this spiritual approach to produce in our legislators an equanimity of temperament, as the peace of God that transcends understanding guarded their hearts.[40]

I knew my small contribution had been assisted not only by the inspiration of God's Word and his Holy Spirit, but also by the intercessions of the tens of thousands of people of faith who had prayed with and for me.

Over the years, I have learned how to pray with assistance, as the opening verses of this chapter, Matthew 18:19-20, recommend. I have found this to be an important step on the journey to learn how to make our voices heard in heaven.

2

PRAY THE
MODEL PRAYER

*The prayer that is born of meditation upon the Word of God is the
prayer that soars upward most easily to God's listening ear.*

R. A. TORREY, *HOW TO PRAY*

I begin this chapter with an important suggestion: Energize your prayer life by starting with the model prayer that Jesus gave to his disciples in Matthew 6, when they asked him to teach them how to pray. In some traditions, this is known as the Lord's Prayer. Others refer to it as the "Our Father."

Why this particular prayer? Well, consider that it was given to us by Jesus himself, who is now in heaven interceding on our behalf. "Because Jesus lives forever, his priesthood lasts forever. Therefore he is able, once and forever, to save those who come to God through him. He lives forever to intercede with God on their behalf."[1] He also "understands our weaknesses, for he faced all the same testings we do, yet he did not sin."[2]

So what did Jesus teach his disciples about prayer?

First, he urged them to pray in secret. "When you pray, go into your room and shut the door and pray to your Father who is in secret. And your Father who sees in secret will reward you."[3] Perhaps because prayer involves the longings of the heart, revealing the secret recesses of the human spirit, we should expose them in private to God. Prayer is more an act of the heart than the lips, and our hearts are best exposed in secret places.

Jesus certainly set the example. Mark reports, "Before daybreak the next morning, Jesus got up and went out to an isolated place to pray."[4] We also know that, on the night he was betrayed, Jesus brought his three closest companions—Peter, James, and John—into the garden of Gethsemane, where he asked them to tarry and pray while he walked further to the inner recesses of the garden for solitary communication with his Father.[5] When Jesus finished his prayer, Matthew 26:40 tells us, "He returned to the disciples and found them asleep. He said to Peter, 'Couldn't you watch with me even one hour?'" Jesus often went up into the mountains to pray alone at night—sometimes all night.[6] He has left us a sterling example of the *power* of secret prayer.

Another reason for praying in secret: We may have private sins to confess that should only be heard by God. When we are alone with God in his sacred throne room, we can be totally transparent with those things that no human ear should hear. And we can be comfortable unburdening our souls to God. As Ecclesiastes 12:14 reminds us, "God will judge us for everything we do, including every secret thing, whether good or bad." This verse suggests that God already knows our secrets, so we can open ourselves completely to him.

We have secret dreams that we want to become reality, and it's important to keep some dreams private. In Matthew 17, Jesus gives an important command to Peter, James, and John as they come down the mountain after the transfiguration experience: "Don't tell anyone what you have seen until the Son of Man has been raised from the dead."[7]

After the angel Gabriel told Mary that she would be the mother of our Savior, and after this message was confirmed by a group of shepherds who came to see Mary and her child after their own encounter with a host of angels, Luke 2:19 reports Mary's response: "Mary kept all these things in her heart and thought about them often."

In the Old Testament, if Jacob's son Joseph had kept his dreams of preeminence to himself, perhaps he might have lived a less complicated life. Perhaps his brothers wouldn't have become jealous and sold him into slavery.[8]

Fortunately, in the secret chambers of solitary prayer, we can tell God everything. We can even talk to him about our secret temptations and ask him for strength to bear what no one else knows but him. With some of our secrets, we are like the disciple Peter attempting to walk on water. When he started to sink, he cried out, "Save me, Lord!"[9] Someone who is beginning to sink usually knows it before anyone else. Only Peter and Jesus knew about his secret fears, and Jesus rescued him in this time of challenge and testing.

We should also pray in secret because it promotes meditation and heart-searching scrutiny, particularly when we pray the Scriptures. We're able to experience the supernatural power of God revealed in the Bible. Hebrews 4:12 says, "The word of God is alive and powerful. It is sharper than the sharpest two-edged sword, cutting between soul and spirit, between joint and marrow. It exposes our innermost thoughts and desires." Exposed to the power of Scripture, we are able to meditate and examine our hearts. Perhaps this is what David was seeking when he cried out, "Search me, O God, and know my heart; test me and know my anxious thoughts."[10] What a blessing is this secret, one-on-one encounter with God.

Our Father in Heaven

The model prayer taught by Jesus began to make a difference in my life when I stopped thinking of it as a prayer to *recite* and began to see it as a prayer to *pray*, using its themes of *adoration*, *confession*, *thanksgiving*, and *supplication*. Starting with the opening words, *Our Father*, I began to react to the feelings and emotions engendered by those simple words. Having grown up without a stable adult male role model in my home, recognizing God as my Father brings me great comfort and peace. It is a privilege to be a part of his family, and it usually takes me about ten minutes or more just to unpack my feelings about those two words.

I follow this strategy for the rest of the prayer—focusing in turn on God's holiness, God's Kingdom, God's will, God's provision, God's forgiveness, and God's deliverance—usually taking about thirty minutes or so to pray it. Each time I pray this prayer, my response is different; it is indeed a transformative and inspirational prayer. When I use it to prime the pump of my conversation with God, I give my celestial Father the honor of directing the dialogue. This greatly increases the likelihood that my prayers will be heard in heaven. Try *praying* instead of merely *saying* this model prayer, and see what you experience.

I have three sons, whom I love, and I enjoy nothing more than conversing with them. That's why I love to call God "my Father" because it establishes my relationship with him. I'm astounded that he permits me to enter his throne room—at any moment of any day—as one of his adopted children. In 1 John 3:1 (NKJV) we are reminded, "Behold what manner of love the Father has bestowed on us, that we should be called children of God!" This is an amazing relationship to have with our omnipotent Creator.

The knowledge that God is my heavenly Father also gives me a sense of peace, a knowledge that eviscerates my worries, obligations, rules, regulations, expectations, and demands, for he directs my steps. Three times before my thirteenth birthday, my family was evicted from our home. But with each eviction, I never doubted that my mother would find another place for my siblings and me to stay. If my love and confidence in an earthly parent can impart to me that kind of peace, imagine the transformative impact produced by a similar filial affection for an all-powerful and all-loving God. The impact brings a peace that transcends human understanding. "Then you will experience God's peace, which exceeds anything we can understand. His peace will guard your hearts and minds as you live in Christ Jesus."[11]

When I think of God as my Father, it brings feelings of great gratitude, providing fuel for my prayers. Philippians 4:6 tells us, "Don't worry about anything; instead, pray about everything. Tell God what you need, and thank him for all he has done." And 1 John 3:2 says, "We are already God's children, but he has not yet shown us what we will be like when Christ appears. But we do know that we will be like him, for we will see him as he really is." If our status as children of God doesn't engender gratitude, what will?

The fact that God is my Father in heaven gives me a cosmic perspective; I realize that I am a pilgrim and sojourner in this world. In 1 Peter 2:11-12, we find these words: "Dear friends, I warn you as 'temporary residents and foreigners' to keep away from worldly desires that wage war against your very souls. Be careful to live properly among your unbelieving neighbors. Then even if they accuse you of doing wrong, they will see your honorable behavior, and they will give honor to God when he judges the world."

Jesus intended for us to have this cosmic perspective. In John 14:2 (NKJV), he says, "In My Father's house are many mansions," where he would go to prepare a place for believers . . . and where he will be waiting for us. Likewise, the apostle Paul admonishes us to set our affections on things above: "Think about the things of heaven, not the things of earth."[12] When I think of my Father in heaven, "the things of earth . . . grow strangely dim, in the light of his glory and grace."[13] I know that I am connected to a power that transcends human limitations.

When Elisha was attacked by enemy soldiers and the young man who accompanied him was fearful, the prophet prayed, "O LORD, open his eyes and let him see!"[14] That prayer was heard in heaven. The young man was able to see a host of angels protecting him and Elisha. These celestial beings weren't tethered by human limitations. Our heavenly Father has resources that empower us beyond our limitations, doing for us "more than we can ask or imagine."[15]

Hallowed Be Your Name

My reverential awe for God motivates me to honor his name. He is sovereign and deserves my best efforts, for I must not besmirch my celestial family name. During my US Navy years, when our ship would pull into a foreign port, the commanding officer would remind the ship's company that, when we went ashore, we represented America, and people would judge our country by our behavior.

It is recorded that Alexander the Great said to a boy who bore his name, "Remember, your name is Alexander." Alexander expected the boy to refrain from doing anything that could stain or tarnish the name. Our connection to God, and our appreciation for the fact that we have become members of his family, should motivate us to try to live with honor, for the glory of his name.

When I think of my celestial family name, it gives me a greater hunger for holiness. After all, my heavenly Father is holy, so shouldn't I strive to be like him? This hunger makes me more aware of my sinfulness and my need for divine power. I then reach out and claim the promise of God's Word: "Blessed are those who hunger and thirst for righteousness, for they shall be satisfied."[16]

Your Kingdom Come

Because I'm a member of God's family, his priorities become mine. I want my life to advance his Kingdom, not mine—and his Kingdom is not of this world.[17] When my behavior doesn't adequately represent his Kingdom, I should desire to change what I'm doing. I make my decisions based on which choice better advances the priorities of my heavenly Father's Kingdom.

At this point in my life, I prefer staying at home to travel. Having spent twenty-seven years in the US Navy, I've traveled more than most. In spite of my reluctance to travel, I know that my Father's Kingdom business requires it of me. His Great Commission challenges me with these words: "Go and make disciples of all the nations, baptizing them in the name of the Father and the Son and the Holy Spirit. Teach these new disciples to obey all the commands I have given you. And be sure of this: I am with you always, even to the end of the age."[18] I believe that God expects me to take advantage of the many invitations I receive to go to other countries and talk about Christ. His Kingdom priorities must be more important than my own.

When I pray "Your Kingdom come," it motivates me to accept God's rule in my life. Both the apostle Paul and the apostle Peter referred to themselves as slaves of Jesus Christ.[19] In 2 Peter 1:1, Peter writes, "I am writing to you who share the same precious faith we have. This faith was given to you because of the justice and fairness of Jesus Christ, our God and Savior." This is the spiritual posture of someone who knows he is not his own. A slave has no rights. When God rules my life, I should realize that I'm his servant. This is why Paul suggested we should think of ourselves as "servants of Christ and stewards of the mysteries of God."[20] Work to ensure that God's Kingdom will rule.

Your Will Be Done on Earth as It Is in Heaven

When I petition God to accomplish his will on earth as it is in heaven, I'm acknowledging that he wants what is best for my life. In Jeremiah 29:11, God tells us he has plans to give us a future and a hope. Are you willing to trust God with your future and live for his will? We should not be reluctant to pray the prayer that Jesus prayed in the garden of Gethsemane, "Not my will, but yours, be done."[21]

The secret to fulfillment in life and maximizing our possibilities is found in staying within the circle of God's will. This is essentially what Jesus is admonishing us to do in Matthew 6:33: "Seek the Kingdom of God above all else, and live righteously, and he will give you everything you need." To seek first God's Kingdom simply means that we desire his will to be done on earth as it is in heaven.

Give Us This Day Our Daily Bread

"Give us this day our daily bread" means to focus on the present and lift up to God our needs, not our greed. We're asking for bread, not caviar. We're trusting God for one day at a time, for "today's trouble is enough for today."[22] Deuteronomy 33:25 (NIV) provides reassurance: "Your strength will equal your days."

Forgive Us Our Debts as We Forgive Our Debtors

We're taught to pray for forgiveness, but our personal forgiveness is connected to our willingness to forgive. Luke 11:4 puts it this way, "Forgive us our sins, as we forgive those who sin against us." We pray for forgiveness because God has promised to give us this gift—if we're willing to confess our need. First John 1:9 says, "If we confess our sins to him, he is faithful and just to forgive us our sins and to cleanse us from all wickedness." Isn't that a wonderful promise? We simply have to confess our sins, and God is willing to forgive us.

We also need to pray for forgiveness to provide us with a fresh start and a clean slate. At the beginning of each year, many people make New Year's resolutions. They rejoice in the fact that they can put the past behind them and start fresh. The New Year is actually an arbitrary boundary; we can start fresh at any time. When we come to God confessing our sins, he cleanses us, providing us with a new beginning. What an amazing blessing.

We pray for forgiveness with the awareness that this blessing should motivate us to show a similar mercy and forbearance to others. How can we possibly refuse to forgive when we think about the enormity of everything for which we have already been forgiven?

Lead Us Not into Temptation

We're taught to pray, "Lead us not into temptation."[23] Temptation is not only seduction to do evil, but it also involves being tested. For people of faith, we have the expectation that God is directing our paths, but we need to build a fence to protect us from sin. Temptation is the open gate through which we do not want to be led. We need protection against temptation because of perils seen and unseen. Satan is our enemy, and he seeks to destroy us. Our greatest protection against him begins with a healthy respect for his powers, which in turn compels us to put on the full armor of God.[24]

God graciously forgives us when we confess our sins, keeping us as members of his family. This should awaken in us an appreciation and reciprocal love that prompts us to avoid even the appearance of evil.[25]

Avoiding temptation, of course, is the first line of defense against sinful habits and addictions. The apostle Paul puts it this way: "You say, 'I am allowed to do anything'—but not everything is good for you. And even though 'I am allowed to do anything,' I must not become a slave to anything."[26] This verse provides us with the wise admonition to avoid things that do not hasten our spiritual progress or that may become addictive. If something isn't good for us, it's probably slowing us down. If we risk becoming enslaved to something, it's probably addictive.

We need to ask God to help us avoid the cruel consequences of sin. Romans 3:23 tells us that "everyone has sinned; we all fall short of God's glorious standard." Sinning and falling short of God's glory may involve life-and-death issues. How wise is the individual who prays with sincerity, "Don't let us yield to temptation, but rescue us from the evil one."[27]

Deliver Us from Evil

Inevitably, in spite of our best efforts, temptations come. That is when we must pray and ask God to "rescue us from the evil one."[28] Sometimes we are blindsided by temptation or its evil twin: *fear*. We're like Peter warming himself by the fire just before denying Jesus.[29] Because of fear, Peter denied Jesus three times, trying to appear uninvolved.

Though Satan is strong and wily, we would do well to remember that God is all-powerful. And he promises to deliver us from evil. In 1 Corinthians 10:13, we find a wonderful encouragement:

> The temptations in your life are no different from what others experience. And God is faithful. He

will not allow the temptation to be more than
you can stand. When you are tempted, he will
show you a way out so that you can endure.

This passage provides a blueprint for escaping the traps
of the devil. It reminds us that the tests we face are common; we are not alone in our struggle against evil. These
verses also help us see that God has already weighed the
temptation and will not permit us to be tempted beyond
our power to resist. Remember, when we cry out to God in
prayer, he has already planned a way to deliver us from evil.

Isn't that great news? For every test we face, God will
provide a way of escape so that we will be able to endure
and prevail. In short, he will rescue us from temptation
to evil. What an amazing blessing! God provides for the
tested and tempted. With spiritual discernment, we can
find God's way of escape. But Paul also offers a warning.
"People who aren't spiritual can't receive these truths from
God's Spirit. It all sounds foolish to them and they can't
understand it, for only those who are spiritual can understand what the Spirit means."[30]

The Kingdom, the Power, and the Glory Belong to God

Prayer that will be heard in heaven is about *God's* Kingdom,
not ours. It's about *God's* glory, not ours. It's about *God's*
power, not ours. This model prayer from Jesus reminds

us that we're responsible for honoring God's Kingdom and doing his will, allowing him to fulfill his purpose for our lives, in our generation and beyond. Thank God for this pattern prayer that enables our voices to be heard in heaven.

3

PRAY WITH PURITY

God blesses those whose hearts are pure, for they will see God.

MATTHEW 5:8

Because sin can block our access to God, it's critical that we learn to pray and live with purity. The Bible reminds us that those who regard iniquity in their hearts will not be heard in heaven.[1] Purity has to do with not being mixed up or adulterated with improper substances or materials. It means that what you see is what you get. We should strive for purity because Jesus was pure, and we seek to follow him. He challenges us to deny ourselves, take up our cross, and follow him.[2] Jesus was able to say about himself, "The ruler of this world . . . has no power over me."[3] Though Jesus "faced all of the same testings we do, yet he did not sin."[4] So for us to pray and live with purity, we must strive for ethical congruence and consistency, reflecting the character of Jesus.

Proverbs assures us that God "delights in the prayers of the upright."[5] And the prophet Isaiah says that God waits for us to come to him "so he can show [us] his love and compassion."[6] Furthermore, "he will be gracious if you ask for help. He will surely respond to the sound of your cries."[7]

We should have such confidence that God wants to answer our prayers that we resonate with the sentiment of 1 John 5:14-15: "We are confident that he hears us whenever we ask for anything that pleases him. And since we know he hears us when we make our requests, we also know that he will give us what we ask for." God is ready and eager to respond positively to our requests, even as earthly parents delight in giving good gifts to their children.[8]

Praying *without* purity hinders our prayers, perhaps because our motives are selfish. James 4:3 states, "Even when you ask, you don't get it because your motives are all wrong—you want only what will give you pleasure." Praying, "O Lord, won't you buy me a Mercedes Benz" is not apt to move the hand of God on our behalf.[9] To pray with purity, we must pray unselfishly.

For a time, when my wife and I were looking for a home near Washington, DC, we made house hunting a full-time job. We prayed and gave God the specifics of what the house should have: granite countertops, upgraded windows, and a gas fireplace. You know, the necessities of life—and beyond.

As long as we prayed about what we wanted, nothing happened. We couldn't find a satisfactory place. Finally, in desperation, we changed our tune, left out the specifics, and just prayed for wisdom. When we stopped praying selfishly, telling God everything we thought we needed, we wound up finding our dream home.

If we desire to pray with purity, we must strive to keep ourselves pure. First Thessalonians 5:22 says, "Stay away from every kind of evil." Even when an action isn't wrong, if it *appears* wrong, we shouldn't do it. When I was receiving ethics training as a new rear admiral in the US Navy, the instructor gave us one succinct rule for living above suspicion: "If you have to explain it, don't do it."

If we desire to live and pray with purity, we must also value and safeguard our souls. In Mark 8:36, Jesus asks, "What do you benefit if you gain the whole world but lose your own soul?" Are you guarding your soul? Are you taking seriously the eternal consequences of moral missteps? The Bible tells us that any husband who mistreats his wife, for example, will hinder his own prayers.[10] An important part of safeguarding our souls is striving to "put to death the sinful, earthly things lurking within" us.[11] We must intentionally prune from our lives those habits and addictions that make us unlike Christ. Perhaps this is what Paul has in mind when he tells the Philippians, "Work hard to show the results of your salvation, obeying God with deep reverence and fear."[12]

Finally, to pray with purity, we must make no provision for our carnal nature. "Instead, clothe yourself with the presence of the Lord Jesus Christ. And don't let yourself think about ways to indulge your evil desires."[13] We must make sure we're not providing a stimulus for evil within our hearts, devising or cherishing provisions to gratify our desires. Get rid of the stashes, the reservoirs. Seek to put on the attitude that John the Baptist had toward Jesus when he said, "He must become greater and greater, and I must become less and less."[14] That's the key to living and praying with purity. When we exalt Christ and humble our own hearts, we'll find ourselves praying with a purity of heart that will enable us to see God and make our voices heard in heaven.

How to Pray with Purity

1. Keep yourself pure.
2. Value and safeguard your soul.
3. Make no provision for your carnal nature.

4
PRAY FEARLESSLY

There is no fear in love, but perfect love casts out fear.
1 JOHN 4:18, ESV

As chaplain of the United States Senate, I'm often intimately aware of the concerns, needs, and fears of our lawmakers and the many others who work on Capitol Hill. I need divine guidance and wisdom to pray prayers each day that will be heard in heaven. As I look out my office window at the Washington Monument, the reflecting pool, and the Lincoln Memorial, I ask God to guide me with invocations and benedictions that will contribute to the harmony, wisdom, and success of the Senate. I depend on God to empower me to pray courageously and without fear.

All people of faith should learn to pray without fear. We should also empower others to live and pray without fear. The Bible teaches that all believers are members of a royal priesthood, equipped to intercede and make our voices heard in heaven.

> You are a chosen people. You are royal priests,
> a holy nation, God's very own possession. As a
> result, you can show others the goodness of God,
> for he called you out of the darkness into his
> wonderful light.[1]

People of faith must be prepared to arm themselves and others against fear. As you think about various weapons, remember that the most effective ones are spiritual. The apostle Paul puts it this way: "We use God's mighty weapons, not worldly weapons, to knock down the strongholds of human reasoning and to destroy false arguments."[2] Paul also says, "Don't worry about anything; instead, pray about everything. Tell God what you need, and thank him for all he has done."[3] When we're tempted to feel anxious and fearful, we should pray instead. By sharing biblical truths, and by living according to what we believe, people of faith can empower others to cast away fear and pray fearlessly.

What are some truths that can help us pray without fear?

We can pray without fear because fear does not come from God. Second Timothy 1:7 tells us that "God has not given us a spirit of fear and timidity, but of power, love, and self-discipline." On the other hand, every good and perfect gift *does* come from God.[4] At its best, fear is an imperfect "gift" foisted upon us by our enemy, the devil.

A second truth that will help us pray without fear is to remember that God is always with us. In Psalm 23:4, David declares, "Even when I walk through the darkest valley, I will not be afraid, for you are close beside me. Your rod and your staff protect and comfort me." And in Hebrews 13:5 (ESV), God promises, "I will never leave you nor forsake you." The presence of God in our lives should be a reminder that we encounter no challenge alone. As Jesus told his disciples just before he ascended into heaven, "Be sure of this: I am with you always, even to the end of the age."[5]

A third truth: God's divine presence is not only *with* us, but he is there to *help* us. Hebrews 13:6 puts it this way: "We can say with confidence, 'The LORD is my helper, so I will have no fear. What can mere people do to me?'" God is more than a passive presence in our lives. He is an active Helper, who both empowers us and guides us. He is not a dispassionate observer as we grapple with frightening and challenging circumstances; instead, he remains "our refuge and strength, an ever-present help in trouble."[6] As he tells us in Psalm 50:15, "Call on me when you are in trouble, and I will rescue you, and you will give me glory."

The apostle Paul even tells us *how* God will help us: "This same God who takes care of me will supply all your needs from his glorious riches, which have been given to us in Christ Jesus."[7] This is an amazing promise. It's a reminder to me that if something is missing in my life, God will eventually supply it—or I don't really need it.

Another reason to pray without fear: God commands us to live our lives without anxiety. Philippians 4:6-7 puts it this way: "Don't worry about anything; instead, pray about everything. Tell God what you need, and thank him for all he has done. Then you will experience God's peace, which exceeds anything we can understand. His peace will guard your hearts and minds as you live in Christ Jesus." God would not command us to do something without enabling us to do it. The Bible challenges us not to be anxious about anything. By God's grace, this can be accomplished.

We can obey God's command to come boldly and fearlessly before his throne, and he promises us grace and mercy in return.[8] In 1 Peter 5:6-7, we find these words: "Humble yourselves under the mighty power of God, and at the right time he will lift you up in honor. Give all your worries and cares to God, for he cares about you." Therefore, we can depend on God, who loves us better than we love ourselves, to help us in our times of need. The burdens that weigh us down will not tax or weary God.

What results can we expect to see from our fearless prayers? First, our prayers can motivate people to be more willing to trust God to direct their lives. As it says in Proverbs 3:5-6, "Trust in the LORD with all your heart; do not depend on your own understanding. Seek his will in all you do, and he will show you which path to take."

This wonderful passage provides a blueprint for conquering fear. It reminds us that when we passionately trust God, seeking his will in all we do, he will guide us. Like the GPS systems we use to navigate our vehicles—which overlook our mistakes and patiently recalculate new routes to get us to our destinations—God's guidance serves as a "godly positioning system." We can conquer our anxiety and pray fearlessly for God to direct our lives, because his word is a lamp to guide our feet and a light for our paths.[9]

Second, our fearless praying should motivate other people to allow God to become their ally. We don't even have to pray for ourselves, for the Holy Spirit articulates to heaven the deepest longings of our hearts.

> The Holy Spirit helps us in our weakness. For example, we don't know what God wants us to pray for. But the Holy Spirit prays for us with groanings that cannot be expressed in words. And the Father who knows all hearts knows what the Spirit is saying, for the Spirit pleads for us believers in harmony with God's own will. And we know that God causes everything to work together for the good of those who love God and are called according to his purpose for them.[10]

Imagine the great advantage these promises afford. No matter what season of life we're in, God is at work for our good. We don't have to be intimidated by the Goliaths we encounter in life, for the battle belongs to the Lord.[11]

Third, our fearless intercession can produce a "perfect love" to immunize others against fear. We see this in 1 John 4:18: "Perfect love expels all fear." This is the key to confronting and vanquishing our fears; we must teach people to embrace God's perfect love. As John writes earlier in the same epistle, "Dear friends, let us continue to love one another, for love comes from God. Anyone who loves is a child of God and knows God. But anyone who does not love does not know God, for God is love."[12] When we love God, our affection for him crowds out fear, destroys trepidation, and enables us to live free of condemnation.[13] We do not dread being punished by an angry God, for he has already demonstrated his great and perfect love for us with the gift of eternal life.[14] As we better understand the true nature of God's unconditional and perfect love, fear disappears.

Perfect love inoculates us against fear by solidifying our relationship with God and with one another. The apostle John describes his experience: "Dear friends, since God loved us that much, we surely ought to love each other. No one has ever seen God. But if we love each other, God lives in us, and his love is brought to full expression in us."[15] Galatians 5:14 (NIV) says that when we love our neighbor as ourselves, we fulfill God's entire law.

Finally, our fearless intercession should help people

make God the foundation of all of their hopes. As David declares in Psalm 27:

> The LORD is my light and my salvation—
> > so why should I be afraid?
> The LORD is my fortress, protecting me from danger,
> > so why should I tremble?
> When evil people come to devour me,
> > when my enemies and foes attack me,
> > they will stumble and fall.
> Though a mighty army surrounds me,
> > my heart will not be afraid.
> Even if I am attacked,
> > I will remain confident.
>
> The one thing I ask of the LORD—
> > the thing I seek most—
> is to live in the house of the LORD all the days of my
> > > life,
> > delighting in the LORD's perfections
> > and meditating in his Temple.
> For he will conceal me there when troubles come;
> > he will hide me in his sanctuary.
> > He will place me out of reach on a high rock.
> Then I will hold my head high
> > above my enemies who surround me.

At his sanctuary I will offer sacrifices with shouts of
    joy,
        singing and praising the LORD with music. . . .

Teach me how to live, O LORD.
    Lead me along the right path,
        for my enemies are waiting for me. . . .
Yet I am confident I will see the LORD's goodness
    while I am here in the land of the living.[16]

Later, the psalmist questioned himself and then gave an
answer to his own query in Psalm 42:5-6, "Why am I discouraged? Why is my heart so sad? I will put my hope in
God! I will praise him again—my Savior and my God!"
There is no need for our souls to be cast down with fear
when we make God the foundation of all of our hopes.

When we place our hope in God and pray without
fear, we're depending upon the power that guides the gal-
axies. William Cullen Bryant, looking up and watching
waterfowl migrate south, penned these lines in his poem
"To a Waterfowl" to remind us that we can place our hope
in the unfolding of God's loving providence:

He who, from zone to zone,
guides through the boundless sky thy certain flight,
in the long way that I must tread alone,
will lead my steps aright.

What a marvelous declaration that the God who guides nature is the one in whom we have placed our hope.

Martin Luther, the sixteenth-century German reformer, captured the notion of placing our hope in God during fearful times with his powerful hymn, "A Mighty Fortress Is Our God." Luther's lyrics illuminate the darkness of fear and inspire us to be more than conquerors, no matter what, and to pray without fear in all of life's seasons:

> *A mighty fortress is our God, a bulwark never failing;*
> *Our helper He, amid the flood of mortal ills prevailing:*
> *For still our ancient foe doth seek to work us woe;*
> *His craft and power are great, and, armed with cruel hate,*
> *On earth is not his equal.*
>
> *And though this world, with devils filled, should threaten to undo us,*
> *We will not fear, for God hath willed His truth to triumph through us:*
> *The Prince of Darkness grim, we tremble not for him;*
> *His rage we can endure, for lo, his doom is sure,*
> *One little word shall fell him.*

If we remember who we are as people of faith, we can teach others to pray without fear, rejoicing in God's perfect love.

How to Pray Fearlessly

1. Trust God to direct your life.
2. Make God your ally.
3. Embrace God's perfect love.
4. Make God the foundation of your hope.

5

PRAY WITH EFFECTIVENESS

For a long while I was a mistress of the art of praying for God to
change difficult circumstances. It took years before I learned how to
pray for God to change me in the midst of the difficult circumstances.

KAREN BURTON MAINS

With all the news of congressional disagreements and discord you see in the media, you may not realize that many individuals on Capitol Hill regularly seek to make their voices heard in heaven through intercessory prayer. Each week that the US Senate is in session, twenty to thirty senators, from both sides of the aisle, meet for a prayer breakfast that begins and ends with prayer. During the closing prayer, lawmakers join hands. Imagine that. One senator made this observation: "It's difficult to join hands and pray with a colleague and then go up to the chamber and figuratively stab him or her in the back." He quickly added, "It's not impossible, but it's difficult."

Also, each week that the Senate is in session, lawmakers

from both sides of the aisle meet for Bible study, which also begins and ends with prayer. If the apostle Paul observed that there were saints in Caesar's household,[1] why wouldn't we expect there to be morally, spiritually, and ethically fit people on Capitol Hill? Why wouldn't we expect the people who make our laws to pray and seek God's perspective and guidance? Why wouldn't we believe that members of the legislative branch and their staffers strive to fellowship with one another, learning biblical principles and discovering how to make their voices heard in heaven? Furthermore, why can't all people of faith become constructive change agents by making their voices heard in heaven?

In Matthew 6:10, Jesus teaches that we should pray for God's will to prevail. If Jesus encourages us to make such a petition a priority in our prayers, perhaps we should comply. It would be pointless for him to encourage us to pray that way if our intercession had no positive effect. In Matthew 5:44, Jesus challenges his disciples to even pray for their enemies and for those who persecute them. His desire is for all people of faith to do likewise. Perhaps prayer has a much greater impact than we imagine.

But what does prayer really accomplish? Some would say that if prayer has any effect at all on what happens, then God's plan must not have been fixed in the first place. What is the relationship between human effort and divine providence? Prayer is a solemn request or an offer of thanksgiving to God, or to another object of worship. It involves making devout appeals to a superior being. The Bible teaches that, in many cases, God works in partnership with humanity.[2] One of the great privileges, therefore, accorded to people of faith is to make their voices heard in heaven by cooperating with divinity. In fact, God commands it. In 1 Thessalonians 5:17, Paul tells us, "Never stop praying." What an amazing command. Prayer is the only thing that people of faith are told to do continuously. This of course doesn't mean spending all day and night on your knees, never sleeping. But as I mentioned earlier, it refers to cultivating an awareness of God's presence and his all-seeing eye. Nothing we do or say is hidden from God's providential love. When I'm taking a long automobile trip with my wife, not a minute of that ten- or fifteen-hour journey passes without my being aware that Brenda is in the car with me. With practice, we can develop a similar awareness of God's omnipresence. When we do, it becomes a form of continuous prayer.

We should also strive to make our voices heard in heaven because such intercession will keep us from missing some of God's choice blessings. As James 4:2 reminds us, "You want what you don't have, so you scheme and kill to get it. You are jealous of what others have, but you can't get it, so you fight and wage war to take it away from them. Yet you don't have what you want because you don't ask God for it." Some blessings hang on the silken cords of prayer. These blessings are given by request only. Who among us wants to risk missing God's blessings because we failed to ask for them? For example, Luke 11:13 tells us that God is willing to give his Holy Spirit to anyone who will ask. What an amazing blessing! But we must ask. God has also promised to give us wisdom upon request.[3] How tragic to go through life with a wisdom deficit because we failed to make our request for it heard in heaven.

Know this: Prayer releases God's power. James 5:17 says, "Elijah was as human as we are, and yet when he prayed earnestly that no rain would fall, none fell for three and a half years!" Imagine one man releasing that kind of power. Are you limiting God's power in your life by failing to make your voice heard in heaven? What if Elijah had simply resigned himself to the status quo? We can have a positive impact on our society, nation, and world by making our voices heard in heaven, thereby releasing God's mighty power.

We should strive to make our voices heard in heaven because such intercession exposes us to the power of God's Spirit interceding on our behalf. You see, prayer is not a matter of bringing isolated pressure on a God who is remote from us; instead, it may be the action of God's Spirit using us for his own glory. If God's Spirit is praying for us, our voices are certainly being heard in heaven, for he is there. What a blessing to have someone praying for us who knows our hearts better than we do. It's like having a skilled advocate pleading for us in a court of law.

Intercessory prayer reminds us that all people are deeply interconnected, and this interdependence is truly known only in God. John Donne put it this way:

> No man is an island, entire of itself; every man
> is a piece of the continent, a part of the main; if
> a clod be washed away by the sea, Europe is the
> less, as well as if a promontory were, as well as if
> a manor of thy friend's or of thine own were; any
> man's death diminishes me, because I am involved
> in mankind; and therefore never send to know for
> whom the bell tolls; it tolls for thee.[4]

Dr. Martin Luther King, Jr., in his famous letter from the Birmingham city jail, expresses this same sentiment of interconnectedness like this: "We are caught in an inescapable network of mutuality, tied in a single garment of destiny."[5] Even in Jesus' model prayer, the "Our Father," we find the plural pronoun used throughout. "Give *us* this day *our* daily bread, and forgive *us our* debts, as *we* also have forgiven *our* debtors. And lead *us* not into temptation, but deliver *us* from evil."[6] When we make our voices heard in heaven, it helps us to remember that we're navigating through this life's journey together.

Intercessory prayer enables us to follow Jesus' example

and walk as he walked.[7] Jesus prayed at all the important events in his all-too-brief, thirty-three-year life. He prayed at his baptism.[8] Before selecting his apostles, he prayed all night long.[9] He rose before daybreak to pray[10] and prayed at the Last Supper before his death.[11] Jesus prayed with thanksgiving,[12] and he interceded for his enemies while on the cross.[13] His first and last words during his crucifixion were prayers. Before he ascended into heaven, he uttered his great intercessory prayer in John 17—"Father, . . . I have given them the glory you gave me, so they may be one as we are one."[14] Repeatedly and fervently throughout his life, Jesus made his voice heard in heaven. If we're to follow his example, we must bathe our lives in prayer.

Remember God's promise in 2 Chronicles 7:14: "If my people who are called by my name will humble themselves and pray and seek my face and turn from their wicked ways, I will hear from heaven and will forgive their sins and restore their land." What a wonderful promise! If a nation is in need of healing and unity, people of faith can make a positive difference in bringing such a metamorphosis to pass. They simply need to approach God with fervency and humility, turning from evil. He then promises to hear them. Yes, their voices will be heard in heaven, bringing the gifts of forgiveness and healing to their land. This Bible promise provides us with a strategy for national revival and renewal.

To summarize, the Bible gives us at least seven reasons to motivate us to make our voices heard in heaven:

1. Intercession is commanded by God.
2. Intercession keeps us from missing blessings.
3. Intercession releases God's power.
4. Intercession exposes us to the power of God's Spirit praying for us.
5. Intercession reminds us of humanity's interconnectedness.
6. Intercession enables us to follow Jesus' example.
7. Intercession can bring healing to any nation.

It's important to remember that we do not always receive what we ask for when we pray. Three times in the garden of Gethsemane, Jesus prayed for his Father to remove the cup of suffering, but God didn't.[15] In 2 Corinthians 12:7-9, the apostle Paul thrice asks God to remove a thorn in his flesh, but God refuses to remove Paul's pain, simply stating, "My grace is sufficient for you, for my power is made perfect in weakness."[16] But even when our prayers aren't answered, we can receive reassurance from Isaiah 55:8-9: "'My thoughts are nothing like your thoughts,' says the LORD. 'And my ways are far beyond anything you could imagine.'" God knows what is best for our lives. Even when he doesn't grant our requests, he is nonetheless working all things together for our good.[17]

First Timothy 2:1-4 provides us with guidance:

I urge you, first of all, to pray for all people. Ask
God to help them; intercede on their behalf, and
give thanks for them. Pray this way for kings
and all who are in authority so that we can live
peaceful and quiet lives marked by godliness
and dignity. This is good and pleases God our
Savior, who wants everyone to be saved and to
understand the truth.

This wonderful Bible passage provides a blueprint for
making our voices heard in heaven through intercessory
prayer.

First, pray from a sense of need. God invites us to
make our voices heard by praying from the depths of our
need.[18] In Luke 18:10, Jesus says, "Two men went to the
Temple to pray. One was a Pharisee, and the other was a
despised tax collector." The Pharisee stood off by himself
and prayed with arrogance, but the tax collector prayed out
of a sense of need: "God, have mercy on me, a sinner."[19]
God heard and answered his prayer. In Philippians 4:19,
we're told that God will supply all our needs. In Psalm
50:15, he invites us to come to him with our problems
and difficulties: "Call on me when you are in trouble, and
I will rescue you, and you will give me glory."

Nehemiah provides a wonderful example; few people have prayed more effectively than he did.

In late autumn, in the month of Kislev, in the twentieth year of King Artaxerxes' reign, I was at the fortress of Susa. Hanani, one of my brothers, came to visit me with some other men who had just arrived from Judah. I asked them about the Jews who had returned there from captivity and about how things were going in Jerusalem.

They said to me, "Things are not going well for those who returned to the province of Judah. They are in great trouble and disgrace. The wall of Jerusalem has been torn down, and the gates have been destroyed by fire."

When I heard this, I sat down and wept. In fact, for days I mourned, fasted, and prayed to the God of heaven. Then I said,

"O LORD, God of heaven, the great and awesome God who keeps his covenant of unfailing love with those who love him and obey his commands, listen to my prayer! Look down and see me praying night and day for your people Israel. I confess that we have sinned against you. Yes, even my own family and I have sinned! We have sinned terribly by not obeying the commands, decrees, and regulations that you gave us through your servant Moses.

"Please remember what you told your servant Moses: 'If you are unfaithful to me, I will scatter you among the nations. But if you return to me and obey my commands and live by them, then even if you are exiled to the ends of the earth, I will bring you back to the place I have chosen for my name to be honored.'

"The people you rescued by your great power and strong hand are your servants. O Lord, please hear my prayer! Listen to the prayers of those of us who delight in honoring you. Please grant me success today by making the king favorable to me. Put it into his heart to be kind to me."[20]

What an amazing and effective prayer. After Nehemiah arrived in Jerusalem, he and the people were able to rebuild the city walls in fifty-two days. Praying with a God-honoring fervency, he reminded God of his promises; he confessed individual and collective sins; he prayed with adoration and thanksgiving, and with reverence and specificity; and his prayer was heard in heaven.

Second, make your voice heard in heaven by praying to God alone. King Hezekiah learned how to do this. While he was king of Israel, he was attacked by Sennacherib, an Assyrian monarch. Sennacherib was so confident he would defeat Israel that he offered King Hezekiah two thousand horses if the Israelite king could find soldiers to put on them.[21] When Hezekiah received this message, he went into the synagogue and prayed to God alone. His prayer is recorded in Isaiah 37:16-20:

> O LORD of Heaven's Armies, God of Israel, you
> are enthroned between the mighty cherubim! You
> alone are God of all the kingdoms of the earth.
> You alone created the heavens and the earth. Bend
> down, O LORD, and listen! Open your eyes,
> O LORD, and see! Listen to Sennacherib's words of
> defiance against the living God.
>
> It is true, LORD, that the kings of Assyria have
> destroyed all these nations. And they have thrown
> the gods of these nations into the fire and burned
> them. But of course the Assyrians could destroy
> them! They were not gods at all—only idols of
> wood and stone shaped by human hands. Now,
> O LORD our God, rescue us from his power; then
> all the kingdoms of the earth will know that you
> alone, O LORD, are God.

King Hezekiah knew what Sennacherib did not: There is only one God to whom we should direct our prayers, and that God is more powerful than any deity crafted by human hands.

When we keep a Godward focus—a God-alone focus—our voices will be heard in heaven, and all the glory will be God's and God's alone.

Third, we're to pray with intimacy. God, our heavenly Father, wants us to have intimate communion with him, which enables us to have blessed intimacy and communion with one another. When I was younger, I heard someone in church remind us that, in reciting the Lord's Prayer, we never once say *I*. We never once say *my*. Neither can we pray the Lord's Prayer without praying for one another. For when we ask for *our daily bread*, we must include our brothers and sisters. Every petition we make involves other people as well as ourselves. From beginning to end, the Lord's Prayer guides us to pray with an unselfish intimacy.

In Acts 26:14, the apostle Paul (aka Saul of Tarsus) gives the testimony of his conversion and his first intimate encounter with God: "We all fell down, and I heard a voice saying to me in Aramaic, 'Saul, Saul, why are you persecuting me? It is useless for you to fight against my will.'" Saul of Tarsus spoke at least three languages, but God spoke to him in the intimacy of his boyhood tongue, Aramaic.

How poignant to observe the intimacy of the prayers of Jesus from the cross. He prayed, "Father, forgive them, for they know not what they do."[22] He quoted Psalm 22:1: "My God, my God, why have you abandoned me? Why are you so far away when I groan for help?" He also prayed Psalm 31:5 when he said, "I entrust my spirit into your hand. Rescue me, LORD, for you are a faithful God." Jesus made his voice heard in heaven by praying with intimacy.

Fourth, we must pray with thanksgiving. In 1 Thessalonians 5:18, we are admonished to "be thankful in all circumstances, for this is God's will for you who belong to Christ Jesus." This verse makes it clear that a part of God's will for our lives is that we express gratitude in every circumstance. We find a similar encouragement in Philippians 4:6: "Don't worry about anything; instead, pray about everything. Tell God what you need, and thank him for all he has done." Psalm 34:1 offers additional guidance: "I will praise the LORD at all times. I will constantly speak his praises."

Fifth, pray for those who govern. We're told to pray "for kings and all who are in authority so that we can live peaceful and quiet lives marked by godliness and dignity."[23] Even when people of faith live under governments they don't approve of, as they did in the first century, they can and should pray for those in power because God is interested in the salvation of all people. In 1 Peter 2:17, we're told, "Respect everyone, and love the family of believers. Fear God, and respect the king." When Peter wrote these words, Nero probably was the emperor. Nonetheless, early members of the church prayed for those who governed. Such intercession should help us resonate with the sentiments of Proverbs 21:1: "The king's heart is like a stream of water directed by the LORD; he guides it wherever he pleases."

Finally, pray with the reinforcement of a quiet and holy life. God doesn't encourage us to strive for martyrdom. Romans 12:18 enjoins, "Do all that you can to live in peace with everyone." Romans 12:1 encourages us to present our bodies as living sacrifices, not dead ones. In Daniel 1, Daniel and his friends negotiated with King Nebuchadnezzar's chief steward, working out a win-win outcome for a challenging problem. We should support our sacred petitions with the ethical congruence of quiet and holy lives. In fact, 2 Corinthians 3:2 (ESV) describes us as "letter[s] of recommendation . . . to be known and read by all." People should be able to read our actions and thereby celebrate our praise for God. Such praise should be the harvest of a quiet and holy life.

Psalm 5:12 has it right: "You bless the godly, O LORD; you surround them with your shield of love." Psalm 84:11 makes this promise: "The LORD will withhold no good thing from those who do what is right." Isaiah 54:17 adds, "No weapon turned against you will succeed." Romans 8:38-39 (CEV) proclaims, "Nothing in all creation can separate us from God's love for us in Christ Jesus our Lord!"

I cannot end this chapter without reminding you of these words of Jesus, spoken to people of faith: "Ask me for anything in my name, and I will do it!"[24] As the book of

Hebrews says, "He lives forever to intercede with God on [our] behalf."[25] Our voices will always be heard in heaven when we allow our Savior, Jesus, to speak on our behalf.

On Capitol Hill, months before the 2016 presidential election, several hundred people decided to fast and pray about who would lead our nation's executive branch. This prayer group included lawmakers, senior and junior staffers, and many others who work in the US Senate. Because this was a bipartisan group, we chose not to pray for a specific candidate, but we made our voices heard in heaven and prayed that God's will would be done. To ensure that our request was sincere, we scheduled a praise and thanksgiving service to follow the election.

Obviously, in any election, different people vote for different candidates, and no matter what the outcome is, there will always be those who are happy and those who are disappointed by the results. Depending on which side you're on, it can be difficult sometimes to discern how God's will could be advanced by a particular candidate's victory. But as we see in the book of Job, God has both an ideal will and a permissive will. He sometimes permits things to happen, knowing that he can bring positives even from negatives.[26]

On the evening of the post-election thanksgiving service, as I walked toward the auditorium, I thought again about God's words in Isaiah 55:8-9: "'My thoughts are nothing like your thoughts,' says the LORD. 'And my ways are far beyond anything you could imagine. For just as the heavens are higher than the earth, so my ways are higher than your ways and my thoughts higher than your thoughts.'" I wondered how many people would attend the gathering, but when I arrived, I was gratified to see that the seats were mostly full and some people were standing around the perimeter. Collectively, we had made our voices heard in heaven through intercessory prayer, and now we had come together again to thank God for his prevailing providence.

United in purpose, we praised God. We sang "Great Is Thy Faithfulness" and other praise hymns because we were convinced that God had heard and answered our prayers. One of the great privileges of being people of faith is that we are able to make our voices heard in heaven.

How to Pray with Effectiveness

1. Pray from a sense of need.
2. Pray to God alone.
3. Pray with intimacy.
4. Pray with thanksgiving.
5. Pray for those who govern.
6. Pray with the reinforcement of a quiet, holy life.

6

PRAY TO ESCAPE THE SQUEEZE OF TEMPTATION

It's always good to keep the Lord between you and Satan.

JON COURSON

Oscar Wilde once observed, "I can resist anything except temptation." Many of us feel the same way. We find temptation difficult to overcome, particularly when it provides a vehicle for our favorite transgressions. But that's reason enough to pray to escape its squeeze.

As Jesus taught, "Don't let us yield to temptation, but rescue us from the evil one."[1] He's encouraging us to nip sin in the bud.

Of course, we can also learn from the mistakes of others—especially not to repeat the mistakes of our Bible heroes and heroines. In 1 Corinthians 10:11, Paul challenges us to avoid the kinds of mistakes—and consequences— that afflicted the nation of Israel in the wilderness after the

Exodus: "These things happened to them as examples for us. They were written down to warn us who live at the end of the age." In Acts 10:34-35, Peter says, "I see very clearly that God shows no favoritism. In every nation he accepts those who fear him and do what is right."

What happened to people in the Bible can happen to us. If we don't learn a lesson from their missteps, we can experience the same punishments and bitter harvests that they did. In speaking of the end times, Jesus said, "The world will be as it was in the days of Lot. People went about their daily business—eating and drinking, buying and selling, farming and building—until . . . fire and burning sulfur rained down from heaven and destroyed them all."[2] And, he added, "Remember what happened to Lot's wife!"[3] Here was a woman who was being led to safety by an angel but made the mistake of looking back to see what she was leaving behind.

We are warned in 1 Corinthians 10:12, "If you think you are standing strong, be careful not to fall." Too often, when we feel we have mastered a temptation, we find ourselves succumbing to the very same thing. We should live our lives with a spirit of humility, always mindful that if others can fall, so can we. We must avoid the overconfidence of Samson in Judges 16. He played games with Delilah, unaware that he was risking his health and happiness. We must heed the admonition of 1 Thessalonians 5:22: "Stay away from every kind of evil."

Always believe, and keep in mind, that we can trust God to get us through every trial. Paul offers this encouragement in 1 Corinthians 10:13: "The temptations in your life are no different from what others experience. And God is faithful. He will not allow the temptation to be more than you can stand. When you are tempted, he will show you a way out so that you can endure."

Paul's words provide a marvelous blueprint for escaping the squeeze of temptation. He reminds us, first, that every test we experience is common to humanity. We should never think that our struggles are unique. Others are battling the same temptations. No matter how it may seem, you are not the only lonely, unhappy, frustrated, disillusioned, or pessimistic person on the planet. Others experience the same emotions. The enemy of our souls would have us think that nobody knows the trouble we've seen; but that isn't true. Trouble and temptation are common to all.

Paul also encourages us with a reminder that God will not permit us to be tested beyond our powers. He weighs the temptation—the greater the test, the greater the confidence God has in our level of moral and spiritual fitness. When temptation comes, you can rest assured that you have the strength to resist it.

Perhaps an even greater encouragement is Paul's assurance that, for every temptation, God provides a way of escape. The way may not always be clear; it may be covered with cobwebs. But if we exercise spiritual discernment, we will be able to discover it. The fact that we know there's a way out should motivate us to *look* for that way and enjoy the blessing of being victorious over temptation.

However, this is not some sort of automatic pass. We really need to prepare ourselves. As Paul says in 1 Corinthians 9:27, "I discipline my body like an athlete, training it to do what it should. Otherwise, I fear that after preaching to others I myself might be disqualified." We must make our bodies our slaves instead of being enslaved by our desires. What can motivate us to have this kind of discipline is remembering the potentially tragic consequences of yielding to temptation. We do not want to become disqualified as we run the race of life.

One of the most important parts of the body to discipline is the tongue. We must learn to control our words, resisting the temptation to murmur and complain. A complaining spirit can cause us to doubt God's goodness, as the children of Israel did during their journey from Egypt to the Promised Land. Harking back to those days in the wilderness, 1 Corinthians 10:10 warns us about the dangers of grumbling: "Don't grumble as some of them did, and then were destroyed by the angel of death." To escape the potential negative consequences of yielding to temptation, we should learn to control our tongues.

The more words we speak, the more likely we are to sin. Proverbs 10:19 reminds us, "Too much talk leads to sin. Be sensible and keep your mouth shut." The more we talk, the greater the chances that, at some point, we will deviate from honesty and candor. Too many words often lead us across the boundaries of constructive speech and into gossip, grumbling, and pessimism. Those who pray to escape the squeeze of temptation should learn to spare their words. As it says in Proverbs 17:27, "A truly wise person uses few words."

Every time we yield to temptation, we play a game of moral and ethical roulette. Every time we yield to temptation, we dance with potentially catastrophic consequences, risking eternal disqualification. We may also bring pain and suffering to others, collateral damage for our weakness. We can pray to escape the squeeze of temptation and obey the admonition of the hymnist:

> *Yield not to temptation, for yielding is sin;*
> *Each victory will help you some other to win;*
> *Fight manfully onward, dark passions subdue,*
> *Look ever to Jesus, He'll carry you through.*
> *Ask the Savior to help you,*
> *Comfort, strengthen, and keep you;*
> *He is willing to aid you,*
> *He will carry you through.*
> *Shun evil companions, bad language disdain,*
> *God's name hold in reverence, nor take it in vain;*
> *Be thoughtful and earnest, kindhearted and true;*

Look ever to Jesus, He'll carry you through.
  Ask the Savior to help you,
  Comfort, strengthen, and keep you;
  He is willing to aid you,
  He will carry you through.
To him that o'ercometh, God giveth a crown;
Through faith we shall conquer, though often cast down;
He who is our Savior, our strength will renew;
Look ever to Jesus, He'll carry you through.[4]

How to Escape the Squeeze of Temptation

1. Learn from others' mistakes.
2. Live with a humble spirit.
3. Remember that everyone is tempted at times.
4. Search for the escape route God has provided.
5. Practice discipline.
6. Control your tongue.

7

PRAY WHEN GOD IS SILENT

Though dark the way, still trust and pray. The answering time will come.
MARY B. WINGATE

In 1987, my mother was in a coma due to a severe allergic reaction to some medication she had been given. Claiming the promises of James 5:16, I went to the hospital, anointed her with oil, and prayed the prayer of faith for the sick to be restored and her sins to be forgiven—fully expecting her to recover. So when the doctor told me that my mother had died, it startled me. It seemed that God had not held up his end of the bargain.

How do we deal with the silence of God? How do we deal with unanswered prayer? What should be our response when we claim a Bible promise and it doesn't seem to be fulfilled? What should we do when God says nothing? The challenge of unanswered prayer may lead us to experience a dark night of the soul, where we are buffeted by the winds of cynicism and despair. But nearly everyone in their lifetime will encounter what seems to be unanswered prayer.

The truth is, God always answers prayer. He just sometimes doesn't give us the answer we want. The Bible says that God's thoughts are as high above our thoughts as the heavens are above the earth.[1] If we always understood what God is doing, we would be as smart as he is. Sometimes, God doesn't grant our requests because we are asking for something that doesn't even exist. We are like the mother of James and John in Matthew 20, who wanted her sons to have places of honor at the right and left of Jesus in his Kingdom. Jesus gently responded by telling her she didn't know what she was asking, that those seats of honor were chosen by God the Father, not by Jesus. Asking for things we don't know about is so true of much of our intercession.

The first way to deal with unanswered prayer is to make sure we are praying correctly.

One day Jesus was praying in a certain place.
When he finished, one of his disciples said to
him, "Lord, teach us to pray, just as John taught
his disciples."[2]

Notice that they didn't ask him how to teach or how to preach. They never said, "Master, teach us how to heal or how to exorcise demons." Instead, they saw a causative connection between the Lord's prayer life and his power and asked him, "Teach us to pray."

How much do you know about prayer? The apostle Peter says that we "must grow in the grace and knowledge of our Lord and Savior Jesus Christ."[3] A part of this growth involves learning how to pray more effectively. Earlier in the same letter, Peter says, "Make every effort to respond to God's promises. Supplement your faith with a generous provision of moral excellence, and moral excellence with knowledge, and knowledge with self-control, and self-control with patient endurance, and patient endurance with godliness."[4]

What did Jesus teach his disciples about prayer? He told them to pray in solitude and that the Father who sees in secret would reward them openly.[5] Jesus himself set the example: "Before daybreak the next morning, Jesus got up and went out to an isolated place to pray."[6] When we pray in solitude, we are more likely to hear the whisper of God's still, small voice, as the prophet Elijah did on Mount Sinai.

> As Elijah stood there, the LORD passed by, and a
> mighty windstorm hit the mountain. It was such
> a terrible blast that the rocks were torn loose,
> but the LORD was not in the wind. After the
> wind there was an earthquake, but the LORD was

not in the earthquake. And after the earthquake there was a fire, but the LORD was not in the fire. And after the fire there was the sound of a gentle whisper.[7]

Perhaps this is why God admonishes us in Psalm 46:10: "Be still, and know that I am God!" It is perhaps not coincidental that when God spoke to the boy Samuel, the child was resting on his bed.[8] Find a solitary place to pray. Your prayers will be more effective, more likely to bring an answer.

A second way to deal with unanswered prayer is to let our words be few—as Jesus taught his disciples.[9] Prayer involves *listening* as well as speaking. Unfortunately, too many people, when they pray, stay in "transmit" mode. Eli the priest told the boy Samuel, "Go and lie down again, and if someone calls again, say, 'Speak, LORD, your servant is listening.'"[10] Too many of us reverse this sequence and declare, "Listen, Lord, for your servant is speaking."

When Jesus prayed in the garden of Gethsemane, as he headed toward Calvary, he repeatedly uttered a focused and sustained prayer: "Father, if it be possible, let this cup pass from me; nevertheless, not as I will, but as you will."[11] The greater the number of words, the greater the probability of uttering something that is not sanctified. We should heed the wisdom of Proverbs 10:19: "Be sensible and keep your mouth shut." Jesus challenged his disciples not to pray with verbosity or repetitiveness, but with brevity and power.

After we structure our prayer life around solitude and brevity, what should we do when God remains silent? Keep on praying. As 1 Thessalonians 5:17 enjoins, "Never stop praying." Matthew 7:7 resonates with this notion: "Keep on asking, and you will receive what you ask for. Keep on seeking, and you will find. Keep on knocking, and the door will be opened to you." Persistence and perseverance are the keys to breakthrough: continuing to pray even when it seems God is not listening.

We see Elijah's persistence on display in 1 Kings 18:41-45. The prophet wanted an end to a drought that had lasted three and a half years. He prayed and then sent his servant out to see if there were any clouds in the sky. When the servant returned and declared he had seen nothing—no sign of rain—Elijah persevered in prayer. He continued to pray and to send his servant to look for a cloud . . . not two or three or five or six times, but *seven* times. Upon his return the seventh time, the servant declared, "I saw a little cloud about the size of a man's hand rising from the sea."[12] When the sky filled with black clouds, Elijah knew that his perseverance had paid off. When God says nothing, and no sign of an answer appears on the horizon, continue to pray.

When God says nothing, surrender to his will. This is what Jesus did in Gethsemane when he repeatedly declared, "I want your will to be done, not mine."[13]

We should desire God's will to be done because he knows what is best for us. As Romans 8:28 reminds us, God is working for the good of those who love him. How dare the creature tell the Creator what to do. In Isaiah 45:9 (NIV), the prophet puts it this way: "Does the clay say to the potter, 'What are you making?'" We should learn that God's way is best for us; he will never lead us astray when we trust in the unfolding of his loving providence.

Jesus left us an example of surrendering to God's will . . . and he knew what it felt like to experience unanswered prayer. The Bible tells us that Jesus was tempted in every way that we have been tempted: "This High Priest of ours understands our weaknesses, for he faced all of the same testings we do, yet he did not sin."[14] So he understands the anguish of unanswered prayer. Luke 6 tells us that Jesus prayed all night, asking God to guide him in the selecting of his apostles. And yet Jesus chose Judas and Peter and ten other men who would one day forsake him and flee. Jesus did not receive the answer to his prayers that he may have hoped for. Nonetheless, the Savior surrendered to the Father's will.

A third way to deal with unanswered prayer is to avoid praying selfishly. Remember the plural pronouns in the Lord's Prayer in Matthew 6? The "Our Father" is an unselfish prayer.

Perhaps this kind of unselfishness is alluded to in Jeremiah 45:5 (ESV), where we are challenged with these words: "Do you seek great things for yourself? Seek them not." When we avoid praying selfish prayers, we use Jesus as our role model. He is the amazing one who "lives forever to intercede with God on [our] behalf."[15]

When we pray for others, we increase the likelihood that God will not only answer that prayer, but bless us for praying that prayer. As God once said to Abraham, "I will bless those who bless you."[16] Position yourself for greater blessings by praying unselfishly.

Never forget that in prayer, we find an antidote for despair. Luke 18:1-8 illustrates the need for constant prayer and offers an example of diligent persistence.

> One day Jesus told his disciples a story to show that they should always pray and never give up. "There was a judge in a certain city," he said, "who neither feared God nor cared about people. A widow of that city came to him repeatedly, saying, 'Give me justice in this dispute with my enemy.' The judge ignored her for a while, but finally he said to himself, 'I don't fear God or care about people, but this woman is driving me crazy. I'm going to see that she gets justice, because she is wearing me out with her constant requests!'"
>
> Then the Lord said, "Learn a lesson from this unjust judge. Even he rendered a just decision in the end. So don't you think God will surely give

justice to his chosen people who cry out to him day and night? Will he keep putting them off? I tell you, he will grant justice to them quickly! But when the Son of Man returns, how many will he find on the earth who have faith?"

How magnificently Jesus harnessed the power of prayer while dying for our sins on Calvary. When we are tempted to despair, let us—by God's grace—follow the example of Christ and pray. Even when God seems to say nothing, we know he is listening and in due season will answer our prayer.

How to Pray When God Is Silent

1. Make sure you are praying correctly.
2. Pray in solitude.
3. Let your words be few.
4. Be quiet and listen for God's voice.
5. Pray persistently.
6. Surrender to God's will.
7. Avoid praying selfishly.

8

PRAY WHEN YOU DON'T FEEL LIKE BEING GOOD

Prayer is the never-failing resort of the
Christian in any case, in every plight.
CHARLES H. SPURGEON

One day, my wife accompanied me to Capitol Hill. We were in the express lane for a significant portion of the drive, until reality set in and we had to shift to the regular lanes to get lined up for our exit. Almost immediately, we found ourselves in nearly stationary traffic. We were going slowly enough that I began to philosophize about the futility of life itself, and I shared my thoughts with Brenda. Recently, I had been reading the pessimistic philosophy of Arthur Schopenhauer, who says in various ways that life is a mess—that we have desires we seek to satisfy, but the relief is brief and temporary. Schopenhauer suggests several ways to deal with this negative reality, but one of his more important suggestions is that we detach ourselves from desire. No matter what happens, he says, we must learn to say, "I don't care."

By this time, the commute traffic had become so intense that it took nearly half an hour to go half a mile. On top of that, drivers whipping along in the express lane were trying to cut in to gain an advantage at the upcoming exits. I was extremely upset with one lady, who almost caused an accident as she forced her way into our lane.

As I fumed and fulminated, Brenda turned to me and said with a smile, "Remember, 'I don't care.'"

I didn't think that was very funny, and at that moment, I certainly didn't feel like being good. It took all my self-control, and a large measure of my theological training, to keep me from snapping back at Brenda in a discourteous way. I *did* care, and sometimes you just don't feel like being good.

There are at least three reasons why, at times, we may not feel like being good: the world, the flesh, and the devil. Let's start with the world, a place filled with allurements and seductions. In 1 John 2:15-17, the Bible warns us about having an excessive love of the world:

> Do not love this world nor the things it offers
> you, for when you love the world, you do not
> have the love of the Father in you. For the world
> offers only a craving for physical pleasure, a
> craving for everything we see, and pride in our

achievements and possessions. These are not from the Father, but are from this world. And this world is fading away, along with everything that people crave. But anyone who does what pleases God will live forever.

Next, the flesh. David declares in Psalm 51:5, "I was born a sinner—yes, from the moment my mother conceived me." We are born with flammable areas in our lives, and it takes a mere spark to ignite the flame. Jeremiah 17:9 reminds us of that unfortunate truth: "The human heart is the most deceitful of all things, and desperately wicked. Who really knows how bad it is?" In Romans 7:18, the apostle Paul admits, "I know that nothing good lives in me, that is, in my sinful nature. I want to do what is right, but I can't."

As if the world and our own flesh aren't enough to drag us down, we must also deal with the devil. As Peter warns in his first letter, "Stay alert! Watch out for your great enemy, the devil. He prowls around like a roaring lion, looking for someone to devour."[1]

Is it any wonder that we sometimes have no desire to be good? Our will seems like a charioteer with two head-strong horses, each pulling in the opposite direction. We seem to have a civil war going on inside us. What should we do to declare a truce? What should we do when we don't feel like being good? How about pray?

Remembering Daddy

The first reason you should pray when you don't feel like being good is because of your spiritual family connections. You aren't just connected to an earthly family; you now have heavenly connections, as well. When you don't feel like being good, remember who your Father is. Peter offers some helpful encouragement: "Live as God's obedient children. Don't slip back into your old ways of living to satisfy your own desires. You didn't know any better then. But now you must be holy in everything you do, just as God who chose you is holy."[2]

We are God's children. We must not forget our divine connections as we strive to live our lives worthy of the privilege of being adopted into God's forever family. When Jesus taught his disciples to pray, he told them to begin their prayer with the words "Our Father in heaven." When we remember our family connection and the goodness and generosity of our heavenly Father, we will be empowered to respond appropriately, even when we don't feel like being good.

Payday Someday

A second reason you should pray when you don't feel like being good is that, one day, God will judge you with strict impartiality. First Peter 1:17 says, "Remember that the heavenly Father to whom you pray has no favorites.

He will judge or reward you according to what you do. So you must live in reverent fear of him during your time here as 'temporary residents.'" Make no mistake about it: Judgment follows the evil deed as the shadow follows the substance. Hebrews 9:27 warns, "Each person is destined to die once and after that comes judgment." Judgment is inevitable, but because the one who judges you is also the one who redeems you, you can face the impartiality of his scrutiny without fear. Nonetheless, it is good to remember that "God will judge us for everything we do, including every secret thing, whether good or bad."[3]

Just Visiting

A third reason you should pray when you don't feel like being good is because you are simply a sojourner in this world. First Peter 1:7 describes the experience: "These trials will show that your faith is genuine. It is being tested as fire tests and purifies gold—though your faith is far more precious than mere gold. So when your faith remains strong through many trials, it will bring you much praise and glory and honor on the day when Jesus Christ is revealed to the whole world."

When we remember that this world is not our permanent home, it enables us to become less upset about the negativity we encounter.

I heard a story some years ago about a missionary who had served for more than ten years in Africa. He was returning home on a ship that also had President Theodore Roosevelt as a passenger. When they arrived in New York, a great band greeted President Roosevelt and his entourage, but there was no one to meet the missionary. As he took a cab alone to where he would be staying, he offered a silent prayer.

"Lord, it really would have been nice if at least one person had been available to welcome me home."

Very quickly, he felt something in his spirit whisper, *You're not home yet.*

It was a reminder to him that, one day, for people of faith, there will be a grand reunion that will dwarf anything this world can offer. Remember, you are a sojourner in this world. The Greco-Roman philosopher Epictetus said that we should live our lives as if we were at an inn. When you go to a hotel, you don't have to own the building to enjoy it. You are a temporary guest, so live that way. Epictetus also said that we should live our lives as if we were at a banquet, where we are offered trays filled with food and drink. We take the portion we want and let the trays pass along to someone else who can also enjoy the offerings. When you remember that you are simply a sojourner here, it will be easier to follow Epictetus's recommendations and treat life like a hotel or a banquet.

Respectable Price

A fourth reason to pray when you don't feel like being good: You should respect the price that Christ paid for your redemption, as so dramatically described in 1 Peter 1:18-19:

> You know that God paid a ransom to save you from the empty life you inherited from your ancestors. And it was not paid with mere gold or silver, which lose their value. It was the precious blood of Christ, the sinless, spotless Lamb of God.

These verses remind us of our value, for the worth of an object is linked to the price someone is willing to pay for it. That God paid so high a price to save us should motivate us not to disappoint the one who has been so generous.

In the movie *Saving Private Ryan*, many soldiers gave their lives so that Private Ryan could get home safely. Captain John Miller, Ryan's superior, challenged the young soldier with these words: "Earn this." While the gift of salvation cannot be earned, the price Jesus paid to redeem us should prompt us to live worthy of such a sacrifice. This is what is meant when the Bible declares that "Christ's love controls us."[4] The passage continues, "Since we believe that Christ died for all, we also believe that we have all died to our old life."[5] When I think of the price paid for my salvation, it deepens my love and gratitude for Jesus, who saved me from eternal ruin. I will always respect the price he paid.

Love Matters

When I don't feel like being good, I try to pray, because I remember that love matters. This is our most important motivation for living for God. He expects us to live lives of brotherly and sisterly love. In fact, Jesus says, "Your love for one another will prove to the world that you are my disciples."[6] Imagine that. People will know we are Christians not because of our erudition, faith, integrity, or generosity, but because of our *love*. Love is so important that the apostle Paul calls it "a still more excellent way."[7] He goes on to say, "If I could speak all the languages of earth and of angels, but didn't love others, I would only be a noisy gong or a clanging cymbal."[8]

Even martyrdom is no substitute for love. Only obedience, rooted in love, truly pleases God. That's why he gave us the power of choice. Jesus said to us, as free moral agents with the ability to choose, "If you love me, you will keep my commandments."[9] Love is so important that the Bible tells us, "The whole law can be summed up in this one command: 'Love your neighbor as yourself.'"[10] I find that astounding. It amazes me that I can keep the entire law of God simply by focusing on love. This is like reading the CliffsNotes of everything pertaining to ethics and theology. Whenever I am faced with an ethical conundrum, I simply need to ask how it relates to loving my neighbor as myself. With that simple question, I bring the full weight of theological truth to bear on the matter. This is a marvelous tactic . . . when I don't feel like being good.

Fading Flowers

When I don't feel like being good, I still pray, because I remember that the things we cherish are temporary. The apostle Peter writes, "As the Scriptures say, 'People are like grass; their beauty is like a flower in the field. The grass withers and the flower fades.'"[11] So there you have it: The great pharaohs and Caesars who once caused people to tremble in awe or terror are now as useful as fading flowers.

This focus on the transitory nature of life should help us resist temptation as we look forward to the permanent blessings of eternity. The apostle Paul puts it this way: "We know that when this earthly tent we live in is taken down (that is, when we die and leave this earthly body), we will have a house in heaven, an eternal body made for us by God himself and not by human hands."[12] Why would I allow a transitory temptation to jeopardize my eternity?

Jesus has gone on ahead to prepare a home of permanence for you and me. He describes this effort in John

14:1-2: "Don't let your hearts be troubled. Trust in God, and trust also in me. There is more than enough room in my Father's home. If this were not so, would I have told you that I am going to prepare a place for you?" This promise gives me tremendous motivation to live with holiness, especially when I don't feel like being good. As noted in 1 John 3:3, "All who have this eager expectation will keep themselves pure, just as [Christ] is pure."

You may recall Luther Ingram's song that describes a man who doesn't feel like being good. He croons, "If loving you is wrong, I don't want to be right."[13] But when I remember who my heavenly Father is, knowing that he will judge me with strict impartiality, I can be a sojourner in this world while respecting the price paid for my redemption. This will motivate me to love my brothers and sisters as I realize that the temporary things of this earth will grow strangely dim in the glorious light of our eternity with Christ.

How to Pray When You Don't Feel Like Being Good

1. Remember that you are God's child and he is your Father.
2. Think of the coming Day of Judgment.
3. Focus on your eternal, heavenly home.
4. Be grateful for Christ's sacrifice for you.
5. Ask God how you can love your neighbor more.
6. Remember that all life's pleasures are short-lived.

9

PRAY WITH PATIENCE

You have passed through the two hardest tests on the spiritual road: the patience to wait for the right moment and the courage not to be disappointed with what you encounter.

PAULO COELHO

Too many times throughout biblical history, people have given up on a goal or objective—or even themselves, refusing to pray with patience. They have made their move too soon, and the move they've made is one of resignation.

Abraham and Sarah made their move too soon. They couldn't wait for God to give them a miracle child. They decided to help God out. Abraham took Hagar to be the mother of his son Ishmael and complicated God's ideal will for this patriarch and his family. Elijah made his move too soon, telling God, "I have zealously served the LORD God Almighty. But the people of Israel have broken their covenant with you, torn down your altars, and killed every one of your prophets. I am the only one left, and now they are trying to kill me, too."[1] But Elijah had given up too quickly. He had made his move too soon. God would soon send him on a mission to anoint Hazael as king of Aram and Elisha as Elijah's own successor. God also reminds him about 7,000 others in Israel who had not bowed to Baal.[2]

After the death of Jesus, the disciples decided to throw in the towel on their ministry. They forgot what the Lord had said about rising in three days. Peter decided to return to his job as a fisherman, and other disciples followed his lead.[3] But Peter made his move too soon, not praying patiently. Two other disciples, not part of the original twelve, had also given up. They were not praying with patience. They were so discouraged by Jesus' crucifixion that they no longer had any hope. They were walking to a town a few miles from Jerusalem when Jesus joined them. They proceeded to walk with Jesus and didn't even recognize him. Tears had blurred their vision; anguish had clouded their comprehension. They talked to Jesus about the crucifixion. He finally challenged them to believe in the resurrection. Beginning with Moses and taking them through the books of the Prophets, he taught them about the things concerning himself. They still didn't know it was Jesus until they saw his wounded hands when he broke bread with them. They had to learn to patiently wait on God.

Why do we fail to pray with patience?

God's Timing

Perhaps we become weary with God's timing. He's just not moving fast enough for us. Psalm 27:14 encourages us to do just the opposite: "Wait patiently for the LORD. Be brave and courageous. Yes, wait patiently for the LORD."

Spiritual Immaturity

Perhaps we suffer from spiritual immaturity and need to grow. As Paul writes in 1 Corinthians 13:11 (ESV), "When I was a child, I spoke like a child, I thought like a child, I reasoned like a child. When I became a man, I gave up childish ways." Second Peter 3:18 says, "Grow in the grace and knowledge of our Lord and Savior Jesus Christ. All glory to him, both now and forever! Amen."

Fruitless Toil

Perhaps we become discouraged by fruitless toil. We see this kind of impatience in the words of Simon Peter when Jesus suggests that he try fishing in deeper water. "Master, . . . we worked hard all last night and didn't catch a thing. But if you say so, I'll let the nets down again."[4] Luke records what happened next: "Soon both boats were filled with fish and on the verge of sinking."[5] Haven't you felt like giving up when you toiled all night and caught nothing? I challenge you: Refuse to quit. Pray patiently as you continue to wait on the Lord.

Misunderstanding God's Word

Perhaps we don't understand God's Word. It wasn't until after Jesus explained the Scriptures to the disciples on the road to Emmaus that their eyes were opened.[6] They later said to one another, "Didn't our hearts burn within us as he talked with us on the road?"[7] In Romans 12:2, Paul encourages us to embrace the transformative power of God's Word: "Don't copy the behavior and customs of this world, but let God transform you into a new person by changing the way you think. Then you will learn to know God's will for you."

Gain a Proper Perspective

How then can we avoid the spiritual impatience that might prompt us to embrace prayerlessness? We need to gain a proper perspective. Psalm 121:2-4 says, "My help comes from the LORD, who made heaven and earth! . . . The one who watches over you will not slumber. Indeed, he . . . never slumbers or sleeps."

See Obstacles as Opportunities

The apostle Paul learned to see obstacles as opportunities. Writing to the Corinthians about a trip he planned to Macedonia, Paul said, "In the meantime, I will be staying here at Ephesus. . . . There is a wide-open door for a great work here, although many oppose me."[8]

First Samuel 17 tells of a time when a young man named David overcame a giant obstacle to seize an opportunity. War was afoot between Israel and the Philistines, and the giant Goliath was the keystone of the enemy force. David—who was a shepherd, not a warrior, and only visiting the battlefront to deliver some food to his older brothers—asked some of the soldiers he met, "What will a man get for killing this Philistine and ending his defiance of Israel? Who is this pagan Philistine anyway, that he is allowed to defy the armies of the living God?"[9] Actually, there was a ready answer: King Saul had pledged one of his daughters in marriage to whoever might defeat the giant. Not only did David seize the immediate opportunity, but soon enough he would become king of Israel.

Control Your Response

Do not allow yourself to be overwhelmed. Always remember that you have control over your response to life's troubles. As Jesus commands in John 14:1, "Don't let your hearts be troubled. Trust in God, and trust also in me." Jesus never lost control of his ability to respond. Even on Calvary, while nailed to a cross, he prayed patiently for his enemies, took care of his mother, and saved a dying thief. He controlled his response to his life's greatest challenge.

Let Your Love for Christ Bring Inner Strength

The apostle Paul writes in 2 Corinthians, "We know that God, who raised the Lord Jesus, will also raise us with Jesus and present us to himself together with you. . . . That is why we never give up. Though our bodies are dying, our spirits are being renewed every day."[10] Perhaps the greatest way to experience God's strength from within us is to be controlled by our love for Christ. "Either way, Christ's love controls us. Since we believe that Christ died for all, we also believe that we have all died to our old life."[11]

Look Outside Yourself for Divine Power

Look outside yourself for the source of divine strength. David knew that he would need more than a shepherd-boy's strength to be victorious over Goliath. Yet, with that strength, he was able to stand boldly and confidently on the field of battle.

> David replied to the Philistine, "You come to me with sword, spear, and javelin, but I come to you in the name of the LORD of Heaven's Armies— the God of the armies of Israel, whom you have defied."[12]

Psalm 46:1-5 reminds us of the inexhaustible resources available to people of faith:

God is our refuge and strength,
*   always ready to help in times of trouble.*
So we will not fear when earthquakes come
*   and the mountains crumble into the sea.*
Let the oceans roar and foam.
*   Let the mountains tremble as the waters surge!*

A river brings joy to the city of our God,
*   the sacred home of the Most High.*
God dwells in that city; it cannot be destroyed.
*   From the very break of day, God will protect it.*

Look outside yourself for the strength that only God can give.

Renew Your Mind with God's Word

Romans 12:2 shows us how to transform our lives: "Don't copy the behavior and customs of this world, but let God transform you into a new person by changing the way you think. Then you will learn to know God's will for you, which is good and pleasing and perfect." We renew our minds when we expose ourselves to the transformative power of God's Word.

Yes, I have more insight than my teachers,
*   for I am always thinking of your laws.*[13]

Your word is a lamp to guide my feet
and a light for my path.[14]

Expect God to Keep You from Evil

Finally, expect God to keep you from the world's evil. In his final prayer in the upper room with his disciples, Jesus asked his Father to protect us: "I have given them your word. And the world hates them because they do not belong to the world, just as I do not belong to the world. I'm not asking you to take them out of the world, but to keep them safe from the evil one."[15] Although we may not be kept from the forces of the world, isn't it wonderful to know that we will be safeguarded from their negative impact? How blessed we are to live in the world but to be kept safe from the evil one.

How to Pray with Patience

1. Gain a proper perspective regarding life's challenges.
2. See obstacles as opportunities.
3. Control your response to life's difficulties.
4. Let your love for Christ bring inner strength.
5. Look outside yourself for divine power.
6. Renew your mind with God's Word.
7. Expect God to keep you from the world's evil.

10

PRAY WITH CELEBRATION

A little lifting up of the heart suffices;
a little remembrance of God, one act of inward worship,
though upon a march, and a sword in hand, are prayers which,
however short, are nevertheless very acceptable to God.

BROTHER LAWRENCE

When I came home from college, talking continuously about my new girlfriend, Brenda, my mother knew I was serious about that relationship.

"Mom, I've never met anyone like her," I heard myself exclaiming.

"Well, son, I've been praying that God would direct you to find the right partner," my mother responded.

My deep feelings of affection for Brenda gave me something to celebrate and talk about. Similarly, when we grow to love God, we should celebrate his goodness, for he provides us with something to talk about. That spirit of celebration should be reflected in our prayers. One of the best ways, therefore, to make our voices heard in heaven is to pray with celebration.

Why should we celebrate God's goodness with our prayers, witnessing with our words about his power and might? First, we have every reason to celebrate God's goodness. As Lamentations 3:22-25 (ESV) reminds us, "The steadfast love of the LORD never ceases; his mercies never come to an end; they are new every morning; great is your faithfulness. 'The LORD is my portion,' says my soul, 'therefore I will hope in him.' The LORD is good to those who wait for him, to the soul who seeks him."

I think of the food that the nation of Israel received in the wilderness every day as God rained down a honey-flavored wafer for them to consume.[1] He sustained more than one million people for more than four decades because of his loving-kindness and tender mercies. Similarly, we are daily sustained by God, borrowing our heartbeats from him, and depending on him for each new, beautiful sunrise and glorious sunset. Our prayers should reflect our gratitude for this generous God. The Lord's Prayer celebrates the majesty of God: "Our Father in heaven, may your name be kept holy. May your Kingdom come soon. May your will be done on earth, as it is in heaven."[2]

Let me offer five reasons why our prayers should celebrate God's goodness, making our voices heard in heaven. First, his mercies are new every morning. Second, he is a stronghold in the day of trouble. Third, his goodness leads us to repentance. Fourth, he extends to us amazing grace. Fifth, he comforts us to make us comforters.

Stronghold

We should pray with celebration because "the LORD is good, a strong refuge when trouble comes."[3] We should come to God *first*—and right away—not make him our last option. We don't honor him when our first instinct is to turn to some bestselling book, or a professional counselor, or some superstitious ritual, instead of looking to him in prayer.

In Matthew 14:30, Peter cries out in desperation, "Save me, Lord!" He shouted this prayer as he began to sink beneath the waves while walking on water. The other disciples were oblivious to his predicament, for it looked as if he was succeeding. When we're in trouble, we usually realize we're going down before anyone else does. We know when we've lost our footing. Likewise, we know before others do when a particular temptation seems overwhelming to us. But like Peter, we should make crying out to God option number one. Peter didn't wait until he was neck deep in water. May we assume he was heeding the admonition of Psalm 50:15? "Call on me when you are in trouble, and I will rescue you, and you will give me glory."

We honor God when we reach out to him in faith and embrace his promise of deliverance. In so doing, we celebrate his power and might. In Matthew 11:28, Jesus reassures us, "Come to me, all of you who are weary and carry heavy burdens, and I will give you rest." Knowing that God desires to give us peace and sweet rest is a good reason for celebratory prayer and praise.

Repentance

We should pray with celebration because God's goodness leads us to repentance.[4] Where would we be without God's goodness drawing us to himself? It is God's innate goodness that breaks the power of our sinfulness and sets the captives free. Even when the prodigal son was in the far country, he knew he could depend on his father's love. In Luke 15:18, he declares, "I will go home to my father and say, 'Father, I have sinned against both heaven and you.'" This wayward young man seemed to know that he would receive his father's unconditional love in spite of his sinfulness. He was led to return home, motivated by thoughts about his father's goodness.

Do you know that nothing we can do will make God love us any less? His affection is unconditional, independent of anything we do or say. Also, nothing we can do will make God love us more. His passion for us is unreserved and unequivocal, prompting us to return from transgression's far country.

We should celebrate God's goodness with our prayers, blessing him at all times[5] because his mercies motivate us to return home and fill the God-shaped void in our hearts. Our repentance is rooted in God's initiatives.

Grace

We should pray with celebration because God extends to us his amazing grace. "God saved you by his grace when you believed. And you can't take credit for this; it is a gift from God. Salvation is not a reward for the good things we have done, so none of us can boast about it."[6]

John Newton, captain of a slave ship, was a recipient of that splendid grace. Newton wrote the hymn "Amazing Grace" after God answered his prayer during a storm at sea. Newton was convinced he would have perished in that storm, if not for God's divine intervention. By the time the ship reached a safe harbor, Newton had become a person of faith because God had extended amazing grace to him.

Perhaps it was God's amazing grace that prompted the dying thief to cry, "Jesus, remember me when you come into your Kingdom."[7] Perhaps he had overheard when Jesus prayed, "Father, forgive them, for they don't know what they are doing."[8] If Jesus could pray for the people who crucified him, perhaps the thief deduced that he stood a desperate chance as well. He prayed a prayer with celebratory intonations: "Lord, I believe that though you're being crucified, you are a king with a kingdom, so remember me." How amazing that this dying felon saw in Christ the King of kings and Lord of lords.

Comfort for Afflictions

God comforts us in all our afflictions. Should we not also pray with celebration that we may comfort others?[9] I thought I was an effective grief counselor until I experienced the devastating grief of my mother's death, which plunged me into a valley of despair. Miraculously, God joined me in that valley and walked me through it, empowering me to comfort others with the comfort I received from him. I'm a better counselor today because of the comfort God supplied me when I had nowhere else to turn. My prayers today celebrate God walking with me throughout that season of distress and grief, bringing me relief that I can share with others.

So how do we prepare to pray with celebration? First, cultivate reverential awe. Proverbs 1:7 states, "Fear of the LORD is the foundation of true knowledge, but fools despise wisdom and discipline." God is not "the man upstairs." He is the sovereign, omnipotent, omniscient, omnipresent God of the universe, who deserves our adoration and praise. Let every knee bow and every tongue confess that he is sovereign.[10]

In Luke 5, when Jesus challenges Peter to launch out into the deep to catch fish, Peter knows that Jesus is a carpenter, not a fisherman, but still he responds: "If you say so, I'll let the nets down again."[11] God rewarded Peter's obedience, for the nets soon overflowed with fish to the point of breaking. This miracle brought Peter to a moment of reverential awe. Looking at Jesus, he declared, "Oh, Lord, please leave me—I'm such a sinful man."[12] He was saying to Jesus, in a sense, "I'm afraid of your transcendent might and power." Yet Peter could now celebrate the God he could sense was dwelling in Christ.

Second, we can prepare to pray with celebration by cultivating a filial relationship with God. As the apostle John writes in his first letter, "Dear friends, we are already God's children, but he has not yet shown us what we will be like when Christ appears. But we do know that we will be like him, for we will see him as he really is."[13]

This filial relationship is an important complement to reverential awe; it is a gentle reminder that, as God's children, we are wrapped in a blanket of mutuality and tied to a single garment of destiny.

When the prodigal son, nearly dead of starvation, returns home and says to his father, "I have sinned against both heaven and you, and I am no longer worthy of being called your son," how does the father reply? He covers the boy's wretchedness with the best robe he could find and initiates a feast. The prodigal might be covered with the dirt of the pigpen, but he is still his father's child. Though he had been lost, now he is found, and he is welcomed home.

Third, we can prepare to pray with celebration by learning to love God's Word, one of the great gifts he has given humanity. In Psalm 119:97, the psalmist declares, "Oh, how I love your instructions! I think about them all day long." When I was in the navy and deployed away from home for six months at a time, I would receive and memorize my wife's letters. These letters brought me such comfort that they were worth committing to memory. We should have a similar passion for the Bible, God's love letter to humanity. Tragically, most people of faith never read through the entire Bible.

We miss great blessings by failing to have passion for God's Word. As God said to Joshua, "Study this Book of Instruction continually. Meditate on it day and night so you will be sure to obey everything written in it. Only then will you prosper and succeed in all you do."[14] The writer of Psalm 119:99 declares, "I have more insight than my teachers, for I am always thinking of your laws." Don't miss out on God's blessings because of your lack of passion for his Word.

Fourth, as Psalm 105:5 encourages us, "Remember the wonders [God] has performed, his miracles, and the rulings he has given." Psalm 103:2 reminds us to praise the Lord and "never forget the good things he does for [us]."

Once, when Jesus' disciples forgot his marvelous works, he warned them to "beware of the leaven of the Pharisees and Sadducees."[15] They talked among themselves about why he had given them such a warning. They thought it must be because they had no bread on the boat, forgetting that not long ago he had fed more than five thousand people with a young boy's lunch of five barley loaves and two fish.[16] Jesus knew what they were talking about. He turned to them and said, "You have so little faith!"[17] Finally, they began to understand that he was not talking about "the yeast in bread, but about the deceptive teaching of the Pharisees and Sadducees."[18] How easy it is to forget the mercies of God, but we have nothing to fear for the future unless we forget how God has led us in the past.

Think about how God has blessed the United States of America. He brought us through the Revolutionary War when we were fighting a global superpower, encompassed about by seemingly impossible odds. He brought us through the Civil War, enabling America to form a more perfect union. He empowered us to survive two World Wars, extricating us from challenges that seemed beyond our strength. We must prepare to celebrate his goodness with our prayers, for we dare not forget his marvelous works.

Fifth, by preparing to celebrate God's mighty deeds in our prayers, we will become better prepared to talk to people about what God has done. As Psalm 105:1 challenges us, "Give thanks to the LORD and proclaim his greatness. Let the whole world know what he has done." How often do you talk to others about God's mighty deeds? When the young David was told by King Saul that he was too inexperienced to fight the giant Goliath, David talked about God's great deeds, informing the king that God had already delivered him from the clutches of a lion and a bear.[19]

Daniel followed David's example and was unafraid to make known God's mighty deeds to King Darius of the Persian empire. After surviving in a den of lions, Daniel said to the king, "My God sent his angel to shut the lions' mouths so that they would not hurt me, for I have been found innocent in his sight. And I have not wronged you, Your Majesty."[20]

If we don't tell the next generation about God's mighty acts, we're only one generation away from agnosticism. We should make God's marvelous deeds known to all of humanity.

Sixth, we should strive to live with holiness even in unholy surroundings. God challenges us, "You must be holy because I am holy."[21] In every generation, people of faith are challenged to represent God's righteousness, even when it seems contrary to the cultural norm. First Thessalonians 1:6-7 reminds us, "You received the message with joy from the Holy Spirit in spite of the severe suffering it brought you. In this way, you imitated both us and the Lord. As a result, you have become an example to all the believers in Greece." Our personal example of holiness is the most compelling message we can give to the world.

Jesus chose to live in a town that was known for its pathology and sinfulness. When Nathanael heard that Jesus was from Nazareth, he asked with disbelief, "Can anything good come from Nazareth?"[22] We are to follow Jesus' example and manifest integrity and holiness, even though we're surrounded by evil. In fact, we are commanded in Romans 12:2, "Don't copy the behavior and customs of this world, but let God transform you into a new person by changing the way you think. Then you will learn to know God's will for you, which is good and pleasing and perfect." The Bible also says that our lives should be living letters that people can read, for our witness is most compelling when words are not necessary.[23]

Seventh, we should praise God's loving-kindness. This is like a child expressing effusive gratitude to a parent. Celebrate God's loving-kindness in your daily life until the habit permeates your prayers. In Psalm 63:3-4, David is quite passionate about this: "Your unfailing love is better than life itself; how I praise you! I will praise you as long as I live, lifting up my hands to you in prayer."

How passionate are you in your prayers and worship of God? Some of us come from religious traditions that are sedate and cerebral, where spontaneous praise may be discouraged. When was the last time you lifted your hands to bless God in worship or shouted hallelujah in his sanctuary? His loving-kindness sustains us. We should strive to be more demonstrative and passionate in our prayer and worship. If we can be passionate at sporting events, why can't we express some emotion when we worship the God who sustains us? David cries, "What if the LORD had not been on our side when people attacked us? They would have swallowed us alive. . . . Praise the LORD, who did not let their teeth tear us apart!"[24] David used his passion for God's goodness as the prelude to his prayers of praise and celebration.

Finally, we should make our voices heard in heaven by striving to leave a constructive legacy, for we shall not pass this way again. How do you want to be remembered? What legacy do you desire to leave, so that you, once dead, will continue to speak?[25] Psalm 92:12 says, "The godly will flourish like palm trees and grow strong like the cedars of Lebanon." How are you building a legacy of fruitfulness and strength?

Acts 13:36 tells us that David served his generation according to the will of God. That's a fitting legacy for any person of faith. By God's grace, we can learn to pray with celebration as we remember the opportunities that God provides for us to do his will on earth. God could use angels or directly intervene, but instead he gives humanity the opportunity to be colaborers with him in his redemptive outreach.

How to Pray with Celebration

1. Cultivate reverential awe for God.
2. Maintain a filial relationship with God.

3. Learn to love God's Word.
4. Remember God's marvelous works.
5. Make known God's mighty deeds.
6. Live with holiness.
7. Praise God's lovingkindness.
8. Prepare to leave a constructive legacy.

11

PRAY WITH INTIMACY

Look deep, yet deeper, in my heart, and there, beyond
where I can feel, read thou the prayer.

GEORGE MACDONALD

We often don't experience the level of intimacy with God that he desires to have with us because we are unaware of our identity and privileges as God's children. We need to know who we are in Christ. The apostle Peter describes our status in heaven as people of faith: "You are a chosen people. You are royal priests, a holy nation, God's very own possession. As a result, you can show others the goodness of God, for he called you out of the darkness into his wonderful light."[1]

What a special blessing to be part of a chosen people. How wonderful it is to be God's special possession. Furthermore, he calls us his friends. As Paul says in his letter to the Romans, "Now we can rejoice in our wonderful new relationship with God because our Lord Jesus Christ has made us friends of God."[2]

We are so special to God that the hairs of our heads are numbered.[3] We are so special to God that he gave us heaven's choicest gift, his only begotten Son.[4] How could a God who loves us so much not desire intimacy with us? How could we not want to respond by getting to know him better?

The apostle Paul, for one, expressed a passionate desire for this knowledge: "I want to know Christ and experience the mighty power that raised him from the dead. I want to suffer with him, sharing in his death."[5]

The Gift of Redemption

Intimacy with God comes from the blessing of our redemption. Ephesians 1:7 describes this blessing: "He is so rich in kindness and grace that he purchased our freedom with the blood of his Son and forgave our sins." He has *saved* us; that's the bottom line. This redemption also restores our right relationship with God through Jesus Christ: "For God made Christ, who never sinned, to be the offering for our sin, so that we could be made right with God through Christ."[6] This verse simply reminds us that we are given credit for the righteous life of Christ. His life is substituted for ours in the judgment because he has already paid sin's penalty. Who would not want to be intimate with someone who has given us the gift of such sweet redemption?

This freedom that God has purchased on our behalf includes freedom from condemnation, which so often is what the enemy uses to try to bring us down. But Paul assures us that "there is no condemnation for those who belong to Christ Jesus."[7] The thought that God's unconditional love motivated him to redeem us, creates in us a desire for greater intimacy with him.

The Gift of Eternal Life

We should also desire intimacy with Christ because of the blessing of eternal life, as described in 1 John 5:13: "I have written this to you who believe in the name of the Son of God, so that you may know you have eternal life." This verse shows us that God wants us to be certain about our eternal destiny—not just *hoping* for eternal life, but *knowing* that we have it. Jesus made the reality of eternal life very clear to Martha, the sister of Lazarus and Mary, when he said, "I am the resurrection and the life. Anyone who believes in me will live, even after dying."[8]

For people of faith, eternal life begins in the here and now. And it is linked to our intimacy with God. As Jesus says in John 17:3, "This is the way to have eternal life—to know you, the only true God, and Jesus Christ, the one you sent to earth."

The Gift of Inner Peace

Intimacy with Christ brings the gift of inner peace. As Jesus himself said, "I am leaving you with a gift—peace of mind and heart. And the peace I give is a gift the world cannot give. So don't be troubled or afraid."[9] Isn't it wonderful, in a troubled and chaotic world, to have the gift of peace? Does that not prompt you to want to know the giver of that gift more fully? Imagine being able to navigate through life with a spirit of exceptional peace, the kind of peace promised in Philippians 4:6-7: "Don't worry about anything; instead, pray about everything. Tell God what you need, and thank him for all he has done. Then you will experience God's peace, which exceeds anything we can understand. His peace will guard your hearts and minds as you live in Christ Jesus." It is the peace we find in Isaiah 26:3: "You will keep in perfect peace all who trust in you, all whose thoughts are fixed on you!" Keeping our focus on Jesus provides a pathway to deeper intimacy with him.

The Gift of Access

One of my greatest pleasures as a follower of Jesus is to know that I have total access to God's presence. As chaplain of the US Senate, I have some access to key lawmakers . . . who invariably are so busy that it could take hours or even days for me to get on their schedules. But whenever

I need my amazing heavenly Father, he is immediately available to meet my needs. That reality engenders a love and affection that cultivates greater intimacy.

Jesus invites us to this wonderful experience of intimacy. He says in Matthew 11:27, "My Father has entrusted everything to me. No one truly knows the Son except the Father, and no one truly knows the Father except the Son and those to whom the Son chooses to reveal him." We are no longer enemies of God's Kingdom; we are now heirs of his promises. Romans 5:2 talks about our new status as people of faith: "Because of our faith, Christ has brought us into this place of undeserved privilege where we now stand, and we confidently and joyfully look forward to sharing God's glory." We can now come into God's presence without fear but with sanctified boldness. Hebrews 4:16 puts it this way: "Let us come boldly to the throne of our gracious God. There we will receive his mercy, and we will find grace to help us when we need it most."

The Gift of an Advocate

My sense of intimacy with God is heightened by my appreciation for the gift of Christ's advocacy on my behalf. In a sense, I have a lawyer in heaven whose audible voice to the Father enables my voice to be heard. The apostle John give us this encouragement in one of his letters: "My dear children, I am writing this to you so that you will not sin. But if anyone does sin, we have an advocate who pleads our case before the Father. He is Jesus Christ, the one who is truly righteous."[10] Our divine advocate, having lived for a time on earth and having suffered the indignities of persecution, knows exactly how we feel. Hebrews 4:15 describes the intimacy and connection we have with Jesus: "This High Priest of ours understands our weaknesses, for he faced all of the same testings we do, yet he did not sin."

With Jesus as my divine advocate, I feel closer to the Father and the Holy Spirit each day. I thank God for the gifts of redemption, eternity, peace, access, and advocacy that create in me a deeper hunger for intimacy with him, enabling me to make my voice heard in heaven.

How to Pray with Intimacy

1. Thank God for the gift of redemption from your sins.
2. Thank God for the gift of eternal life in heaven.
3. Thank God for the gift of inner peace.
4. Thank God for the gift of immediate access to him anywhere, anytime.
5. Thank God for the gift of our divine advocate, Jesus Christ.

12

PRAY WITH FERVENCY

The more that prayer becomes the untrammeled, free and natural
expression of the desires of our hearts, the more real it becomes.

O. HALLESBY

I once asked my college preaching professor what surprises he had encountered in his long and distinguished academic career. He responded, "Barry, one of the things that has surprised me is that students from great backgrounds often do not succeed as well in life as those who come from challenging and impoverished environments."

As an officer who sat on more than thirty promotion boards in the US Navy, I often found myself thinking about what my professor had said. I, too, found it surprising that many who came from the best schools and made the best grades were not always the ones who received a promotion. Still, I pondered why underachievement so often seemed to be the case among "the best and the brightest," and I was reminded of the words of the poet Longfellow, regarding the blessings that come from extra effort:

> *The heights by great men reached and kept*
> *Were not attained by sudden flight,*
> *But they, while their companions slept,*
> *Were toiling upward in the night.*[1]

Could it be that people with fewer advantages succeed more than those blessed with greater abundance because of greater effort? Perhaps these more successful individuals have also learned to live and pray with fervency.

Why do we sometimes fail to live and pray with all our might? Could it be because it's easier to be lazy? Proverbs 26:13 says, "The lazy person claims, 'There's a lion on the road! Yes, I'm sure there's a lion out there!'" Proverbs also says, "Lazy people take food in their hand but don't even lift it to their mouth."[2]

I once asked a US Senator who was approaching his ninetieth birthday how he continued to write books. He responded, "I don't watch television."

Another reason why we may fail to live and pray with fervency is because we are intimidated by the talents of others. In the parable of the three servants in Matthew 25, the master gives one servant five talents, another servant two talents, and a third servant one talent. It can be intimidating to have one talent and be working next to someone with five. After all, if the five-talent person squanders one, he or she still has 80 percent left. But if we have only one talent and lose it, we've lost everything.

We may fail to live and pray fervently because such effort can bring pain. As Jesus says in John 16:33, "I have told you all this so that you may have peace in me. Here on earth you will have many trials and sorrows. But take heart, because I have overcome the world." So we can expect pain and difficulty in this life—especially when we are putting forth maximum effort. Perhaps this is why we are challenged to follow Jesus by voluntarily choosing suffering: "If any of you wants to be my follower, you must give up your own way, take up your cross, and follow me."[3]

We must strive to live and pray with all our might. Ecclesiastes 9:10 advises, "Whatever you do, do well. For when you go to the grave, there will be no work or planning or knowledge or wisdom." This fervency in living is echoed by the prophet Jeremiah: "This is what the LORD says: . . . 'If you look for me wholeheartedly, you will find me.'"[4] Even in our searching after God, intensity matters. Psalm 42:1 declares, "As the deer longs for streams of water, so I long for you, O God." When we pursue God as a thirsty deer seeks out water, we are beginning to live with all our might.

Another reason we should strive to live and pray with

earnest effort is because life's journey is coming to an end. Jesus knew this about his own life when he said, "We must quickly carry out the tasks assigned us by the one who sent us. The night is coming, and then no one can work."[5] Moses had the same idea when he prayed, "Teach us to number our days, that we may gain a heart of wisdom."[6] Likewise, David numbered his days when he prayed this consoling prayer: "My future is in your hands. Rescue me from those who hunt me down relentlessly."[7] What a comfort to know that our times are in God's hands.

We should live and pray fervently to give God what he is due. He really does want *all* of us. Deuteronomy 6:4-5 declares: "Listen, O Israel! The LORD is our God, the LORD alone. And you must love the LORD your God with all your heart, all your soul, and all your strength." David says, "Honor the LORD for the glory of his name. Worship the LORD in the splendor of his holiness."[8] Yes, God deserves our continuous praise. In Psalm 103:2, David advises, "Let all that I am praise the LORD; may I never forget the good things he does for me." Indeed.

We must live and pray with fervency because others deserve our best efforts. Romans 14:7 observes, "We don't live for ourselves or die for ourselves." You and I are indeed our brothers' (and sisters') keepers.[9] This focus on loving and serving others is also captured in Galatians 5:14: "The whole law can be summed up in this one command: 'Love your neighbor as yourself.'" This is a great insight.

I can fulfill the entirety of God's law simply by loving my neighbors as I love myself.

Never forget, we are accountable to God for our efforts. Second Corinthians 5:10 reminds us, "We must all stand before Christ to be judged. We will each receive whatever we deserve for the good or evil we have done in this earthly body." The knowledge that I must one day appear before the judgment seat of Christ and be weighed in the balance should motivate me to give my best effort.

In the parable of the three servants, the man with only one talent offers an interesting excuse for doing nothing: "Master, I knew you were a harsh man, harvesting crops you didn't plant and gathering crops you didn't cultivate. I was afraid I would lose your money, so I hid it in the earth. Look, here is your money back."[10] That excuse did not work then, and it won't work now. Prepare to have your efforts judged by God.

Yet another reason to live and pray fervently: self-respect. We should respect ourselves enough to do our best. In Nehemiah 6:11, when Nehemiah's enemies told that great man of faith to flee for his life, he responded, "Should someone in my position run from danger? Should someone in my position enter the Temple to save his life? No, I won't do it!"

When we have a healthy respect for who we are and our responsibilities as people of faith, we will strive to live up to our full potential. As Wayne Dyer once put it,

"Don't die with your music still in you."[11] Are you giving the world *all* the music God has placed in you?

The vast majority of valuable work is done not by the most talented people, but by ordinary folks like you and me. What God is looking for are people who are *available* to him. Luke 10:2 reminds us that "the harvest is great, but the workers are few. So pray to the Lord who is in charge of the harvest; ask him to send more workers into his fields." We should, therefore, pray for more laborers, more prayer warriors, more people willing to get involved in putting "love your neighbor as yourself" into action.[12] The wheels of progress move primarily because of the labors and prayers of the less-gifted few who make the effort. So I use fervency in my prayers, joining other one- and two-talent colleagues in making our voices heard in heaven.

God only expects us to faithfully use what he has given us. I can't sing like an angel or preach like Paul, but by God's grace, I can faithfully pray with passion and fervor. Prayer is a wonderful resource available to all. That's why "Jesus told his disciples . . . that they should always pray and never give up."[13]

The apostle Peter made this comment about Paul's writings:

> Our beloved brother Paul also wrote to you with the wisdom God gave him—speaking of these things in all of his letters. Some of his comments

are hard to understand, and those who are
ignorant and unstable have twisted his letters to
mean something quite different, just as they do
with other parts of Scripture. And this will result
in their destruction."[14]

God didn't give Paul and Peter the same number of talents, but he expected them to use their abilities with faithfulness. They had to make the effort.

Jesus repeatedly encouraged people to *try*. In Matthew 12:13, he says to a man with a withered hand, "Hold out your hand." He was asking the man to make the effort, even though the task seemed impossible. Likewise, he said to a lame man who had been at the pool of Bethesda for thirty-eight years, "Stand up, pick up your mat, and walk!"[15] In other words, live fervently; make the effort. He also expects us to make the effort with our prayers, continuously and fervently making our requests known to God.

One of the best strategies I know for those who are seeking to live and pray with all their might is found in Matthew 5:41: "If a soldier demands that you carry his gear for a mile, carry it two miles." Second-mile living is a key to fervency. It will motivate you to "love your enemies, do good to those who hate you, bless those who curse you, and pray for those who spitefully use you."[16] When you go beyond the minimum in using your abilities for God's glory, you will live with exemplary fervency.

No one lived and prayed with more fervency than Jesus. He left behind the chants and songs of angels. He left behind unpolluted breezes and undarkened days. He left his Father's presence and a rainbow-encircled throne in a land where night never comes, making a breakthrough at Bethlehem to save humanity. He went the second mile and beyond. He spent thirty years preparing for a three-year ministry. Isaiah 53:2-5 describes his experience in this way:

> My servant grew up in the Lord's presence like a
>> tender green shoot,
>> like a root in dry ground.
> There was nothing beautiful or majestic about his
>> appearance,
>> nothing to attract us to him.
> He was despised and rejected—
>> a man of sorrows, acquainted with deepest grief.
> We turned our backs on him and looked the other
>> way.
>> He was despised, and we did not care.
>
> Yet it was our weaknesses he carried;
>> it was our sorrows that weighed him down. . . .
> He was pierced for our rebellion,
>> crushed for our sins.

He was beaten so we could be whole.

He was whipped so we could be healed.

With Christ as our leader and head, we have been given a standard of excellence that will enable us, by his grace, to live and pray with all our might, remembering that "the earnest prayer of a righteous person has great power and produces wonderful results."[17]

How to Pray with Fervency

1. Don't give in to laziness.
2. Don't compare yourself to others.
3. Number your days.
4. Give your best to God and to others.
5. Be available and willing to work hard.
6. Practice "second-mile" living.
7. Follow Christ's example.

13

PRAY WITH PERSEVERANCE

The "tendency to persevere," to persist in spite of all hindrances,
discouragements and "impossibilities": it is this that in all
things distinguishes the strong soul from the weak.

THOMAS CARLYLE

When it seems that our prayers go unanswered, we must pray with perseverance and persistence, remembering that God's delays don't mean he has denied our requests. Decades passed between God's promise of Isaac to Abraham and Sarah and its fulfillment; the promise was delayed, but not denied. Joseph spent more than two years in prison before being elevated to Pharaoh's household.[1] The promise was delayed, but not denied. Perhaps the delayed fulfillment of God's response to prayer is seen most graphically in Daniel 10:1-14:

In the third year of the reign of King Cyrus of Persia, Daniel (also known as Belteshazzar) had another vision. He understood that the vision concerned events certain to happen in the future—times of war and great hardship.

When this vision came to me, I, Daniel, had been in mourning for three whole weeks. All that time I had eaten no rich food. No meat or wine crossed my lips, and I used no fragrant lotions until those three weeks had passed.

On April 23, as I was standing on the bank of the great Tigris River, I looked up and saw a man dressed in linen clothing, with a belt of pure gold around his waist. His body looked like a precious gem. His face flashed like lightning, and his eyes flamed like torches. His arms and feet shone like polished bronze, and his voice roared like a vast multitude of people.

Only I, Daniel, saw this vision. The men with me saw nothing, but they were suddenly terrified and ran away to hide. So I was left there all alone to see this amazing vision. My strength left me, my face grew deathly pale, and I felt very weak. Then I heard the man speak, and when I heard the sound of his voice, I fainted and lay there with my face to the ground.

Just then a hand touched me and lifted me, still trembling, to my hands and knees. And the man said to me, "Daniel, you are very precious to God, so listen carefully to what I have to say to you. Stand up, for I have been sent to you." When he said this to me, I stood up, still trembling.

Then he said, "Don't be afraid, Daniel. Since the first day you began to pray for understanding and to humble yourself before your God, your request has been heard in heaven. I have come in answer to your prayer. But for twenty-one days the spirit prince of the kingdom of Persia blocked my way. Then Michael, one of the archangels, came to help me, and I left him there with the spirit prince of the kingdom of Persia. Now I am here to explain what will happen to your people in the future, for this vision concerns a time yet to come."

Harness the Power of the Spiritual Disciplines

What does Daniel's amazing story teach us about praying with perseverance? First, it reminds us to harness the power of the spiritual disciplines. Daniel fasted and prayed. We also see the power and usefulness of fasting in the story of Esther, who fasted and prayed for three days in order to receive an answer to her prayers.[2] Jesus prepared for his encounter with the devil in the wilderness of temptation by fasting and praying for forty days.[3] Striving to master the spiritual disciplines will prepare you to deal with God's delays.

Know that God Hears

We must know that God hears our prayers, even when it seems he is silent. In Exodus 3, Moses encounters God at a burning bush, where God assures him, "I have certainly seen the oppression of my people in Egypt. I have heard their cries of distress because of their harsh slave drivers. Yes, I am aware of their suffering."[4] Israel had been in slavery for four hundred years, but God tells Moses, "I have heard their cries." Regardless of your current circumstances, know that God is listening and that he hears your cries for help.

Expect Spiritual Opposition

Perhaps the most important thing we need to understand about delayed answers to prayer is the reality of demonic opposition. In Daniel's case, the angel who had come to give him the answer he sought had been delayed on his journey. Even though our prayers sometimes seem to go unanswered, we must continue to master the spiritual disciplines, continue to know that we are precious to God, and continue to know that God is listening, even when he is silent. We can expect demonic opposition, but we can also expect God's purposes to always prevail. Galatians 6:9 puts it this way: "Let's not get tired of doing what is good. At just the right time we will reap a harvest of blessing if we don't give up." So cry out to God and keep on asking, seeking, and knocking, because your season of harvest is guaranteed. You may be experiencing a delay, but you have not been denied.

How to Pray with Perseverance

1. Practice the spiritual disciplines of fasting and praying for an extended period of time.
2. Know that God is always listening.
3. Expect demonic opposition.

14

PRAY WITH SUBMISSION

We feel we just don't have the strength to pray as Jesus did;
it seems we're just too needy. And yet that very thing is what
most qualifies us to pray: our weakness, our neediness,
our dependence, our helplessness.

DAVID JEREMIAH

We can pray with submission to fulfill God's will. In the "Our Father," we are taught to make the petition, "Your will be done."[1] If we are to make our voices heard in heaven, we must learn to pray with the perfect submission that Jesus exhibited in the garden of Gethsemane when he said to his Father, "Not as I will, but as you will."[2]

No doubt Joseph prayed that God would permit him to go back home after his brothers threw him in the pit. Instead, God permitted Joseph to go to Egypt as a slave, sold by his brothers to a band of foreigners.[3] Joseph later spoke to his brothers about what they had done to him. "You intended to harm me," he said, "but God intended it all for good. He brought me to this position so I could save the lives of many people."[4] By praying with submission, Joseph opened himself up to be used mightily by God.

When I was younger, I knew I was called to the ministry . . . but I ran from this calling because I felt that being a pastor meant poverty. Every preacher I knew seemed financially challenged. I prayed often about my vocational options, but I did not desire to do God's will. To some extent, I was saying to God, "Not your will but *mine* be done."

Why are we sometimes reluctant to pray with submission, to strive only to fulfill God's will? One reason: We've inherited a sinful nature. As Psalm 51:5 reminds us, "I was born a sinner—yes, from the moment my mother conceived me."

A second reason: We have an enemy who seeks to harm us. We are reminded of this danger in 1 Peter 5:8: "Stay alert! Watch out for your great enemy, the devil. He prowls around like a roaring lion, looking for someone to devour." The devil will do anything he can to interfere in our relationship with God.

A third reason: We are more focused on externals than internals. We forget the wisdom of God's words to his prophet in 1 Samuel 16:7: "Don't judge by his appearance or height, for I have rejected him. The LORD doesn't see things the way you see them. People judge by outward appearance, but the LORD looks at the heart."

We also fail to pray with submission because we refuse to make his purposes a high priority in our lives. This is the opposite of what God wants us to do. In Matthew 6:33, we are challenged by these words: "Seek the Kingdom of God above all else, and live righteously, and he will give you everything you need." God desires for us to make his will our top priority.

We can learn a valuable lesson from the admonition given to us in 1 Peter 4:1-5:

> Since Christ suffered physical pain, you must arm yourselves with the same attitude he had, and be ready to suffer, too. For if you have suffered physically for Christ, you have finished with sin. You won't spend the rest of your lives chasing your own desires, but you will be anxious to do the will of God. You have had enough in the past of the evil things that godless people enjoy—their immorality and lust, their feasting and drunkenness and wild parties, and their terrible worship of idols.
>
> Of course, your former friends are surprised when you no longer plunge into the flood of wild and destructive things they do. So they slander you. But remember that they will have to face God, who stands ready to judge everyone, both the living and the dead.

The first lesson: Make Jesus your example in undeserved suffering. Peter makes it clear that, because Christ suffered physical pain, we should arm ourselves with the same attitude he had and prepare to suffer also. The apostle Paul echoes this theme in 2 Timothy 3:12: "Everyone who wants to live a godly life in Christ Jesus will suffer persecution." Likewise, Isaiah 53:3, 5 gives us a stark description of the suffering of Christ, our role model:

> He was despised and rejected—
>   a man of sorrows, acquainted with deepest grief.
> We turned our backs on him and looked the other
>   way.
>   He was despised, and we did not care. . . .
> He was pierced for our rebellion,
>   crushed for our sins.
> He was beaten so we could be whole.
>   He was whipped so we could be healed.

We can see that the bar has been set high. When we pray for God's will to be done, we can expect some negative circumstances, just as Jesus experienced. Remember what John said about Jesus: "He came to his own people, and even they rejected him."[5]

A second lesson: Embrace the purgative effect of suffering. We are told that those who have suffered physically for Christ have finished with sin.[6] This is great news, a reminder that our willingness to accept God's perfect will, even when it involves suffering, enables us to cultivate a purity that can energize our prayers. The psalmist put it this way in Psalm 119:67: "I used to wander off until you disciplined me; but now I closely follow your word."

A third lesson: Focus your actions on the will of God. When, as a result of suffering, we stop "chasing [our] own desires," we will "be anxious to do God's will."[7] As David declares in Psalm 40:8, "I take joy in doing your will, my God, for your instructions are written on my heart."

We also have the amazing prayer of Jesus in Gethsemane: "Father, if you are willing, please take this cup of suffering away from me. Yet I want your will to be done, not mine."[8] That, my friend, is informing your actions by depending on God to direct your steps; it's the submissive prayer that will be heard in heaven. Do you have the courage to end your prayers by asking for God's will to be done?

A fourth lesson: Remember your sinful past. We have been there, done that, and have the T-shirts of transgression to show for it. When we remember how far God has brought us and how magnificently he has saved us, making us "more than conquerors,"[9] how could we not desire to fulfill his perfect will? David remembered his sinful past, and in Psalm 51:3 declares, "I recognize my rebellion; it haunts me day and night." We, too, will have such memories of missing God's standards of excellence when we hunger and thirst for his perfect will to be accomplished in our lives.

A fifth lesson: Prepare for the coming judgment.

First Peter 4:5 warns us that "we will have to face God," who will "judge everyone." This sentiment resonates with 2 Corinthians 5:10: "We must all stand before Christ to be judged. We will each receive whatever we deserve for the good or evil we have done in this earthly body." Who would not want to pray for God's will to be done? After all, God will be the ultimate judge of our lives. May his Word motivate us to pray with submission for his will to be done on earth through us, even as it is done in heaven.

Pray Biblical Prayers

One of the best ways to pray with submission for God's will to be accomplished is to repeat the prayers of the Bible, praying words that were inspired by the Holy Spirit,[10] prayers guaranteed to be heard in heaven. In Acts 10:34, we're told that "God shows no favoritism." So if God answered a prayer for someone in the Bible, he will, without partiality, respond positively to us when we pray the same prayer.

Perhaps this is the reason why the prayer of Jabez is so popular. I daily read this Bible prayer from 1 Chronicles 4:9-10:

> There was a man named Jabez who was more honorable than any of his brothers. His mother named him Jabez because his birth had been

so painful. He was the one who prayed to the God of Israel, "Oh, that you would bless me and expand my territory! Please be with me in all that I do, and keep me from all trouble and pain!" And God granted him his request.

Think of the power of praying for God's perfect will when you pray this biblical prayer. You are asking God for a daily blessing. You see, not every blessing is a permanent one. You are asking God to keep his hand on you today because you are longing for his presence. You are expressing awareness that life brings trouble and pain from which we can be protected by a sovereign God. Think of the power of asking God to expand your territory, to enlarge your sphere of influence.

This is a powerful biblical prayer to pray. When you pray this prayer, you are praying with submission for God's will to be done. You should look for other prayers in the Bible, print them out, and carry them with you, praying them throughout the day. The book of Psalms is a treasure trove of biblical prayers. When you want to confess your sins, think of the beauty of praying from Psalm 51:

Have mercy on me, O God,
    because of your unfailing love.
Because of your great compassion,
    blot out the stain of my sins.

Wash me clean from my guilt.
    Purify me from my sin.
For I recognize my rebellion;
    it haunts me day and night.
Against you, and you alone, have I sinned;
    I have done what is evil in your sight.
You will be proved right in what you say,
    and your judgment against me is just.
For I was born a sinner—
    yes, from the moment my mother conceived me.[11]

When you pray David's penitential psalm, you are indeed praying with perfection for God's will.

One of my favorite prayers is found in Philippians 1:9-10:

> I pray that your love will overflow more and more, and that you will keep on growing in knowledge and understanding. For I want you to understand what really matters, so that you may live pure and blameless lives until the day of Christ's return.

When I pray this powerful prayer, I am indeed praying God's will. I am asking him to increase my love. This is a wonderful request because it will empower me to fulfill God's great commandment to love. I am also asking him to give me more knowledge and depth of insight. This request resonates with the sentiments of 2 Peter 3:18, which admonishes us to "grow in the grace and knowledge of our Lord and Savior Jesus Christ." This powerful biblical prayer also prepares me for God's scrutiny of my life and cautions me to be pure and blameless until the day Christ returns.

When I pray for God's will, I'm also asking him to provide me with the ability to make the best decisions in my life by understanding what really matters. This will often motivate me to follow the advice of Hebrews 12:1: "Since we are surrounded by such a huge crowd of witnesses to the life of faith, let us strip off every weight that slows us down, especially the sin that so easily trips us up. And let us run with endurance the race God has set before us."

A "weight" is not necessarily a sin. A weight is anything that hinders our progress toward the Kingdom of God. A weight is anything that slows us down. When we learn to make the best choices, we will strip off every weight.

Those who desire to pray with submission to God's will by praying biblical prayers he has already answered will have their voices heard in heaven.

Focus on Heaven

When we pray with submission to God's will, it helps to focus on heaven—for our petition states, "May your will be done on earth, as it is in heaven."[12] We are sometimes reluctant to focus on heaven because of our love for the world. The apostle John warns us about this temptation:

> Do not love the world or anything in the world. If anyone loves the world, love for the Father is not in them. For everything in the world—the lust of the flesh, the lust of the eyes, and the pride of life—comes not from the Father but from the world. The world and its desires pass away, but whoever does the will of God lives forever.[13]

We see in this passage the three trump cards that the devil has in his hand: the lust of the flesh, the lust of the eyes, and the pride of life. The lust of the flesh refers to weaknesses such as gluttony, sexual lust, and laziness. The lust of the eyes highlights the greed we feel when we have an illusion of ownership. Jesus was no doubt thinking about the lust of the eyes when he warned us about laying up treasures on earth.[14] There is also the pride of life, which involves our desire to accomplish and achieve, to be appreciated and accepted. We forget that God is more interested in our faithfulness than in our success or failure. As he says in Revelation 2:10, "Don't be afraid of what you are about to suffer. The devil will throw some of you into prison to test you. You will suffer for ten days. But if you remain faithful even when facing death, I will give you the crown of life."

If, in praying with submission to God's will, we focus on heaven, we will refuse to be discouraged by trouble. The apostle Paul describes it this way in 2 Corinthians 4:18: "We don't look at the troubles we can see now; rather, we fix our gaze on things that cannot be seen. For the things we see now will soon be gone, but the things we cannot see will last forever."

When we focus on heaven as we pray for God's perfect will, we should also see ourselves as representatives of the world to come. In Colossians 3:17, we are told, "Whatever you do or say, do it as a representative of the Lord Jesus, giving thanks through him to God the Father." Do you see yourself as a representative of Jesus Christ? Are you willing to make no decision for which you are not able to ask for Jesus' endorsement? When we want God's will to be done, we will live to honor the name of Jesus.

Finally, when we pray with submission to God's perfect will, with a focus on heaven, we will no longer see death as an enemy. Jesus said these comforting words to Martha: "I am the resurrection and the life. Anyone who believes in me will live, even after dying."[15] Perhaps that is why Paul writes in Philippians 1:21, "Living means living for Christ, and dying is even better." By focusing on heaven, Paul was able to cry out, "O death, where is your victory? O death, where is your sting?"[16]

What a blessed privilege to pray with submission to God's will with a focus on heaven. It enables us to be

God's representatives on earth, living fearlessly because we see death as a defeated foe. It enables us not to be distracted by temptations and troubles as we look forward with confidence to "a city with eternal foundations, a city designed and built by God."[17]

How to Pray with Submission

1. Follow Jesus' example for how to face suffering.
2. Allow suffering to cleanse your soul.
3. Focus on God's will.
4. Remember your sinful past.
5. Prepare for the coming judgment.
6. Pray biblical prayers that God has already answered.
7. Focus on heaven.

15

PRAY WITH A PARTNER

*Where two or three gather together as my
followers, I am there among them.*

MATTHEW 18:20

We began this book by talking about praying with assistance and exploring the "Our Father," the model prayer that Jesus gave us to pray. As you will remember, this pattern prayer helps us to pray patiently and fearlessly with purity, effectiveness, perseverance, intimacy, fervency, and submission. This pattern prayer empowers us to escape the squeeze of temptation, to pray when God is silent, and to pray when we don't feel like being good. These benefits can be enhanced with a final piece of the puzzle: praying with a partner. Praying with a partner will bring fresh power to our prayers, energizing our intercession.

Jesus suggested that this strategy brings exceptional power. He said, "If two of you agree here on earth concerning anything you ask, my Father in heaven will do it for you. For where two or three gather together as my followers, I am there among them."[1]

What does this amazing promise mean? It obviously doesn't mean that we will receive our request every time, no matter what we pray with a partner. For example, we know that James and John, the sons of Zebedee, came to Jesus in agreement and asked him to allow them to sit on his right and his left in the coming Kingdom.[2] But Jesus responded, "You don't know what you are asking!"[3] In order for Matthew 18:19 to be taken literally and without qualification, we would have to ignore the fact that two or three people have agreed to pray on many occasions and yet their prayers were not answered the way they expected. Whenever we pray—alone or with others—we must desire the answer that God, in his wisdom and love, knows best. The power of praying with one or two others lies in our corporate ability to discern God's will. When we pray with others who also are submitting themselves to the will of God, we're less likely to be deceived or to pray foolishly. Praying with a partner positions us to experience God's greater wisdom and love as he choreographs our destinies with his loving providence.

Another reason why we should pray with a partner is to protect our prayers from selfishness. When Jesus taught his disciples to pray, he repeatedly used plural pronouns. This prayer is about *us*, not about *me* or *you* as individuals.

Praying with a partner leads us down an unselfish path, helping to purge our prayers of self-centeredness.

We also should pray with a partner because Jesus is as much present with two people as he is with a very large congregation. In other words, we don't need an entire church praying in order for us to pray with power, making our voices heard in heaven. Jesus Christ, the greatest intercessor, joins in the prayer experience wherever two or three are gathered in his name.[4] In Acts 12, a small group of believers was praying in the home of Mary, and their prayers were powerful enough to get God to send an angel to rescue Peter from prison and certain death. It is this power that is available to people of faith whether their prayer group is large or small.

We should pray with a partner because it brings unity of mind, spirit, and purpose among believers. What could be more unifying than finding common ground with another believer, possessing the same mind, and voicing the same concerns? Here's how Acts 2:1 (NKJV) describes the experience: "When the Day of Pentecost had fully come, they were all with one accord in one place." These people, who were the recipients of the Holy Spirit on the Day of Pentecost, were united in their prayers, and it brought power and results.

Finally, we should pray with a partner because partners can bless and cheer one another. In Luke 10, Jesus sends his disciples out two by two, intending for them to bless and cheer one another. Ecclesiastes 4:9-12 describes the blessings that can come from partnering with others:

> Two people are better off than one, for they can help each other succeed. If one person falls, the other can reach out and help. But someone who falls alone is in real trouble. Likewise, two people lying close together can keep each other warm. But how can one be warm alone? A person standing alone can be attacked and defeated, but two can stand back-to-back and conquer. Three are even better, for a triple-braided cord is not easily broken.

What wonderful blessings are available in partnerships! Paul and Silas discovered these blessings. David and Jonathan discovered these blessings. Release God's power by praying with a partner, making your voices heard in heaven.

How to Pray with a Partner

1. Focus on unselfish prayer requests.
2. Harness the power of praying with another believer.
3. Embrace the unity of corporate prayer.
4. Cheer and encourage your prayer partner.

NOTES

INTRODUCTION
1. Alfred Tennyson, "Morte d'Arthur," *Poems*, 4th edition (London: Moxon, 1845).
2. Romans 4:21
3. Mark 6:2-6
4. Matthew 17:20
5. Psalm 50:15, ESV
6. Author paraphrase.
7. John 17:1-3, author paraphrase.
8. Psalm 100:3
9. John 20:21
10. 1 Peter 5:8, NKJV
11. 1 Timothy 2:1-4
12. Ephesians 3:20

PRAY WITH ASSISTANCE
1. Philippians 1:9-10
2. Psalm 51:5, ESV
3. Romans 7:18
4. Romans 7:24, ESV
5. Psalm 103:14, ESV
6. Luke 22:32, ESV
7. Hebrews 7:25
8. Luke 23:34

9. See Romans 8:26.
10. 2 Peter 3:18
11. Genesis 1:1
12. John 1:3, ESV
13. Proverbs 3:5-6
14. Zechariah 4:10
15. See Esther 4.
16. Luke 5:1-11
17. www.letsrun.com/forum/flat_read.php?thread=1185898&page=1
18. Daniel 1:20
19. Proverbs 27:1, ESV
20. Matthew 20:21
21. Matthew 20:22
22. Ecclesiastes 4:9-10
23. Matthew 18:19
24. See Matthew 6:9-13.
25. Philippians 2:13
26. 1 Samuel 3:10, NIV
27. Isaiah 55:8-9, ESV
28. Luke 23:46, ESV
29. James 1:5
30. James 1:6-8, ESV
31. Psalm 127:1, ESV
32. Psalm 133:1, NIV
33. Philippians 2:3
34. James 1:19
35. 1 Corinthians 3:6
36. Galatians 6:9
37. Genesis 8:22
38. Proverbs 3:6
39. Psalm 22:3
40. See Philippians 4:7.

PRAY THE MODEL PRAYER

1. Hebrews 7:24-25
2. Hebrews 4:15

3. Matthew 6:6, ESV
4. Mark 1:35
5. Matthew 26:36-39
6. Luke 6:12
7. Matthew 17:9
8. Genesis 37
9. Matthew 14:30
10. Psalm 139:23
11. Philippians 4:7
12. Colossians 3:2
13. Helen H. Lemmel, "Turn Your Eyes Upon Jesus" (1922). Public domain.
14. 2 Kings 6:17
15. Ephesians 3:20, NIV
16. Matthew 5:6, ESV
17. John 18:36
18. Matthew 28:19-20
19. See Romans 1:1, 2 Peter 1:1.
20. 1 Corinthians 4:1, ESV
21. Luke 22:42, ESV
22. Matthew 6:34
23. Matthew 6:13, ESV
24. See Ephesians 6:10-17.
25. 1 Thessalonians 5:22, KJV
26. 1 Corinthians 6:12
27. Matthew 6:13
28. Ibid.
29. John 18:18
30. 1 Corinthians 2:14

PRAY WITH PURITY

1. Psalm 66:18, NKJV
2. Matthew 16:24
3. John 14:30
4. Hebrews 4:15
5. Proverbs 15:8

6. Isaiah 30:18
7. Isaiah 30:19
8. Luke 11:13
9. Bob Neuwirth, Janis Joplin, Michael McClure, "Mercedes Benz," copyright © 1970 Universal Music Publishing Group.
10. 1 Peter 3:7
11. Colossians 3:5
12. Philippians 2:12
13. Romans 13:14
14. John 3:30

PRAY FEARLESSLY

1. 1 Peter 2:9
2. 2 Corinthians 10:4
3. Philippians 4:6
4. James 1:17
5. Matthew 28:20
6. Psalm 46:1, NIV
7. Philippians 4:19
8. Hebrews 4:16
9. Psalm 119:105
10. Romans 8:26-28
11. 1 Samuel 17:41-47
12. 1 John 4:7-8
13. Romans 8:1
14. John 3:16
15. 1 John 4:11-12
16. Psalm 27:1-6, 11, 13

PRAY WITH EFFECTIVENESS

1. Philippians 4:22
2. See Matthew 8:5-33, 9:18-22, 14:22-33; Mark 6:5-6.
3. James 1:5
4. John Donne, "Meditation 17," from *Devotions Upon Emergent Occasions* (1624).
5. Martin Luther King, Jr., letter from the Birmingham city jail, April

16, 1963, 2; http://okra.stanford.edu/transcription/document
_images/undecided/630416-019.pdf.

6. Matthew 6:11-13, ESV. Italics added.
7. 1 John 2:6
8. Luke 3:21
9. Luke 6:12
10. Mark 1:35
11. Matthew 26:27
12. John 6:11, 11:41
13. Luke 23:34
14. John 17:21-22
15. Luke 22:42
16. 2 Corinthians 12:9, ESV
17. Romans 8:28
18. Matthew 5:3
19. Luke 18:13, NIV
20. Nehemiah 1:1-11
21. Isaiah 36:8
22. Luke 23:34, ESV
23. 1 Timothy 2:2
24. John 14:14
25. Hebrews 7:25
26. Romans 8:28

PRAY TO ESCAPE THE SQUEEZE OF TEMPTATION

1. Matthew 6:13
2. Luke 17:28-29
3. Luke 17:32
4. Horatio R. Palmer, "Yield Not to Temptation" (1868). Public domain.

PRAY WHEN GOD IS SILENT

1. Isaiah 55:9
2. Luke 11:1, NIV
3. 2 Peter 3:18
4. 2 Peter 1:5-6

5. Matthew 6:6, NKJV
6. Mark 1:35
7. 1 Kings 19:11-12
8. 1 Samuel 3:1-10
9. Matthew 6:7-8
10. 1 Samuel 3:9
11. Matthew 26:39, ESV
12. 1 Kings 18:44
13. Matthew 26:39
14. Hebrews 4:15
15. Hebrews 7:25
16. Genesis 12:3

PRAY WHEN YOU DON'T FEEL LIKE BEING GOOD
1. 1 Peter 5:8
2. 1 Peter 1:14-15
3. Ecclesiastes 12:14
4. 2 Corinthians 5:14
5. Ibid.
6. John 13:35
7. 1 Corinthians 12:31, ESV
8. 1 Corinthians 13:1
9. John 14:15, ESV
10. Galatians 5:14
11. 1 Peter 1:24
12. 2 Corinthians 5:1
13. Homer Banks, Carl Mitchell Hampton, and Raymond E. Jackson, "If Loving You Is Wrong," copyright © 1972 Sony/ATV Music Publishing LLC, Universal Music Publishing Group.

PRAY WITH PATIENCE
1. 1 Kings 19:14
2. 1 Kings 19:15-18
3. John 21:2-3
4. Luke 5:5
5. Luke 5:7

6. Luke 24:13-31
7. Luke 24:32
8. 1 Corinthians 16:8-9
9. 1 Samuel 17:26
10. 2 Corinthians 4:14, 16
11. 2 Corinthians 5:14
12. 1 Samuel 17:45
13. Psalm 119:99
14. Psalm 119:105
15. John 17:14-15

PRAY WITH CELEBRATION

1. Exodus 16:4-5, 31, 35
2. Matthew 6:9-10
3. Nahum 1:7
4. Romans 2:4
5. Psalm 34:1
6. Ephesians 2:8-9
7. Luke 23:42
8. Luke 23:34
9. 2 Corinthians 1:3-4
10. See Philippians 2:10-11.
11. Luke 5:5
12. Luke 5:8
13. 1 John 3:2
14. Joshua 1:8
15. Matthew 16:6, ESV
16. See John 6:1-15.
17. Matthew 16:8
18. Matthew 16:12
19. 1 Samuel 17:32-37
20. Daniel 6:22
21. 1 Peter 1:16
22. John 1:46
23. See 2 Corinthians 3:2.
24. Psalm 124:2-3, 6

25. See Hebrews 11:4.

PRAY WITH INTIMACY
1. 1 Peter 2:9
2. Romans 5:11
3. See Luke 12:7.
4. See Romans 8:32.
5. Philippians 3:10
6. 2 Corinthians 5:21
7. Romans 8:1
8. John 11:25
9. John 14:27
10. 1 John 2:1

PRAY WITH FERVENCY
1. Henry Wadsworth Longfellow, "The Ladder of St. Augustine,"
   The Poetical Works of Henry Wadsworth Longfellow, rev. ed., vol. III
   (Boston: James R. Osgood, 1876), 90.
2. Proverbs 26:15
3. Matthew 16:24
4. Jeremiah 29:10, 13
5. John 9:4
6. Psalm 90:12, NIV
7. Psalm 31:15
8. Psalm 29:2
9. See Genesis 4:9.
10. Matthew 25:24-25
11. https://vimeo.com/19672457
12. See Luke 10:25-37.
13. Luke 18:1
14. 2 Peter 3:15-16
15. John 5:8
16. Luke 6:27-28, NKJV
17. James 5:16

PRAY WITH PERSEVERANCE

1. See Genesis 40–41.
2. See Esther 4.
3. See Matthew 4:1-11.
4. Exodus 3:7

PRAY WITH SUBMISSION

1. Matthew 6:10
2. Matthew 26:39, ESV
3. See Genesis 37:18-28.
4. Genesis 50:20
5. John 1:11
6. 1 Peter 4:1
7. 1 Peter 4:2
8. Luke 22:42
9. Romans 8:37, NIV
10. 2 Timothy 3:16
11. Psalm 51:1-5
12. Matthew 6:10
13. 1 John 2:15-17, NIV
14. See Matthew 6:19-20.
15. John 11:25
16. 1 Corinthians 15:55
17. Hebrews 11:10

PRAY WITH A PARTNER

1. Matthew 18:19-20
2. See Mark 10:35-37.
3. Mark 10:38
4. See Matthew 18:20.

ABOUT THE AUTHOR

Barry C. Black is the only African American admiral in the history of the United States Navy Chaplain Corps. He is also the only African American to be appointed chaplain of the United States Senate. Born into a single-parent home in the inner city of Baltimore, along with seven siblings, he went on to earn doctorates in both ministry and psychology. He has preached on every continent, including Antarctica, and is in great demand as a speaker. He has also written *From the Hood to the Hill*, *The Blessing of Adversity*, and *Nothing to Fear*. Currently, he cares for the spiritual needs of the United States Senate, where he has served as chaplain since 2003. Barry and his wife, Brenda, are the parents of three adult sons and reside in Woodbridge, Virginia.

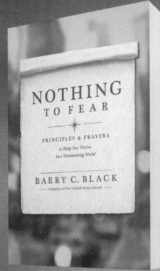

THE **HELP** AND **HOPE** YOU NEED
TO SURVIVE LIFE'S BROKENNESS.

EVERYONE GOES THROUGH SEASONS OF DIFFICULTY.

Dr. Barry Black, chaplain of the United States Senate, has been there too.
Now, in *The Blessing of Adversity*, he shares with you a path to find peace in
the midst of tough times. Discover how to deal with God's seasons of silence,
how to encourage yourself in life's storms, and how to use your pain to help others
through their hardest seasons. No matter your circumstance, the fact remains:

GOD IS WITH YOU.

978-1-4143-2680-1

CP1188